MISMATCHED LUGGAGE

UNPACKING YOUR SEXUAL BAGGAGE FOR YOUR SPIRITUAL JOURNEY

REV. DIANNA RITOLA

Hawthorne Corner

CONTENTS

ACKNOWLEDGMENTS

I would like to thank several people for helping me to bring this book out of my head and into physical reality.

For regular meetings over matzo ball soup and for gentle honest critiques, I am indebted to my writing group: Emily, Avi, and Micki.

For trusting me to hold space for their processes of unfolding and learning, I thank my clients.

For valuable feedback from my beta readers: Sheri, Vajra, Michele, Christina, and Louis.

For listening to my writing process woes and triumphs, I am forever grateful to Shae, Sarah, Lynn, and Dix Marie.

For honest and compassionate advice and a big dose of enthusiasm, I thank my editor, D.A. Sarac, at The Editing Pen.

To my daughters, Ila and Mira, who grew up living in the cauldron of the creation of my work and this book, I thank you for your patience and love and for trusting that by working together, we'd usually figure out the best way through any challenge.

For holding me when I thought I would never finish, for

loving me when I was cranky and frustrated, and for believing in my dreams and my work each and every day, I honor my wife, Michele. As we noted in our wedding ceremony, we each reveal the best in the other.

PREFACE

Sometimes you've got to let everything go—purge yourself. If you are unhappy with anything... whatever is bringing you down, get rid of it. Because you'll find that when you're free, your true creativity, your true self comes out.

—Tina Turner

Welcome! Thank you for opening this book and beginning your examination into the spiritual aspect of your sexuality. I know firsthand how baggage from the past—those denied or repressed parts of yourself that have been keeping your truth locked up in suitcases of shame—can weigh on your heart, mind, and soul and manifest as physical pain or inability to maintain deep relationships.

Left unclaimed, our baggage of shame and pain can hinder us from moving forward diminishing our enjoyment of life. These bags are heavy. They're bulky. They get in the way of connecting with our true selves: our inherent divinity cloaked in our innate humanity.

I'm here to remind you that there is a way to unpack those bags, to examine the programming and assumptions you've been given, to reflect on old hurts, old stories and experiences, and love yourself into wholeness. The key is not to deny the body like some religious and cultural messages say. We are most whole when we live fully in our bodies, loving the skin we're in, and accepting that our body is the vehicle by which we experience everything around us physically and spiritually.

This may sound odd to you if you were raised with the belief that in order to be a spiritual person you had to deny "the flesh" and focus your mind on heaven or God. For many of us, religion and spirituality were mandates through which we were taught to ignore our physical bodies and restrict our human desires for touch and sexual intimacy. Yet ignoring our bodies creates a divide within us that contributes to physical pain and mental and emotional distress because the habit of dismissing bodily sensations sets us up for greater spiritual and psychological pain down the line.

There has been a huge upsurge in the talk of self-love in the past decade or two. Memes and articles circulate on social media about putting yourself first and learning to let go of judgment. Those are fine sentiments, but they don't help much in building a road map for us to find our way out of negative self-talk, diminishing our abilities and desires, and learned codependent behavior.

This road map is one we create for ourselves when we practice affirmative thoughts and actions that remind us of our worth, as I will explain in this book. Self-love leads us into healing our deepest sexual and spiritual pain, releasing the stories and lies that have clouded our thoughts so we can learn to celebrate our sexual, sensual selves and, when we choose, enter into intimate relationships. When we love ourselves and are more available to connect to the unlimited love of the divine, the more love we have to give to others.

No matter where you fall on the spectrum of sexual desire, most humans have an inherent need to touch and be touched. In fact, studies have shown that regular physical contact, both platonic and specifically sensual, reduce the stress hormone cortisol, increase the "connection" hormone oxytocin, and contribute to overall physical, mental, and emotional health. Thinking about sexuality as a part of our whole selves and not just as arousal and sexual intercourse or oral stimulation of genitals leading to orgasm gives us permission to embrace all our desires and name them as parts of our sexual selves.

You and I were made to experience pleasure and joy in our embodiment. Our bodies have billions of sensory nerve endings for hearing, seeing, touching, tasting, and smelling, and they allow us to enjoy sensual pleasure and to share that with other people in myriad interactions throughout life's journey: in casual conversation, holding your child's hand, smelling fresh bread or a garden of flowers, experiencing music and visual art, sexual adventure that affirms you and makes you happy, as well as deeply sharing your body and soul with your lover, life partner, or spouse.

Sometimes this journey will be messy. That's okay. Being human is messy. Having a body, mind, and heart is messy. Too many of us are told throughout our lives "no pain, no gain," as if the pursuit of pleasure and happiness are silly goals that come from an immature understanding of the way the world works. We are culturally programmed to believe that we cannot learn from pleasure, and therefore, it has little value. Yet pleasure is one of the sensations our bodies are designed to feel, and those warm and welcome sensations translate into thoughts and emotions of happiness and well-being. This then improves our health and our relationships and makes us want more.

- If you're tired of feeling stuck in your sexual relationship...
- If you're done with being scared to ask for what you want...

- If you have difficulty expecting that a lover would want to please you...
- If you're exhausted with keeping up appearances while keeping your pain locked away...
- If you hate the thought of hiding your desires from your lover because those desires are too "weird"...
- If you just want to be loved for your whole self and show up as the person you know you are...

Then now is the time to open those bags and satchels and trunks you've been hauling around for who knows how long and dare to peek inside.

What you find may surprise you. There will be opinions of others, cultural strictures, and moral judgments. There will be memories of pleasure, experiences of pain, and religious taboos. You may have secret compartments holding embarrassments and activities that you don't want anyone to know about.

You don't have to keep everything, but this is your opportunity to begin examining the pieces to see if they still fit your life. When you discover what doesn't fit anymore, you can choose to let those beliefs and behaviors go. If your discovery still fits a little or serves a purpose, it will serve you better the more you understand it. Knowing yourself deeply is the key to your connection with your divine self. You may also find that bringing these beliefs, thoughts, and experiences out into the light of day and seeing them from a new perspective allows you to forgive yourself and others for behaviors and actions during those times you didn't know other ways to handle a situation or relationship.

Along the way, I'll be sharing some of my journey, as well as the journeys of some of my clients and some questions to guide you in your own journey. Much of the baggage we tote around as individuals is very similar to the baggage of others. Shame comes when we think that our baggage is too odd, too different, too much, too ugly, too... fill in the blank... to look at or share with someone else. I want you to know that your sexual baggage is no better nor worse than anyone else's. I think you'll identify with some of these stories of unpacking mismatched luggage and reclaiming your body's truth as a spiritual sexual being.

Ready to open the latch? Let's go!

1

MY MISMATCHED LUGGAGE

I've been alive a long time, long enough to know that the more baggage you carry in life, the more unstable you'll be, until eventually you get sick of carrying it, and then you just fall down.
—Rebecca McNutt, *Bittersweet Symphony*

"HOW DID YOU GET TO BE A MINISTER, AND WHY DO YOU FOCUS on sex and intimacy as part of spirituality? Aren't ministers supposed to be in a church?" This comment, or something similar, is often the response I get when someone new to me asks what I do for work. You know the drill: you're at a party or an event where there are several people having the get-to-know-you talk. Introductions of names are made, sometimes with someone doing the intros but more often with self-introduction. "Hi, I'm DiAnna." A few sentences later the other person says, "So, what do you do?"

I usually say, "I'm an interfaith minister and sex educator, offering spiritual counseling and workshops on the intersection of sex and spirituality." Unlike a more traditional job, like lawyer, teacher, or bookstore owner, the title of minister brings up images that often have some strong connotations for the person in front of me. Some express surprise that I am a female minister. Some are unaware that ministry happens outside a church setting. Often the phrase "sex and spirituality" is the cause of the curiosity associated with the above questions.

The answer of how and why is a long story, maybe a series of stories, that has grown out of how I was raised, recognizing wounds and patterns that led to my own search for healing, and who I am now as I continue to unfold into more of my true self. I am not here to write my entire autobiography, but sharing some things about my life with you can help to explain why I wrote this book.

Like any story, there are many events that could be considered a catalyst for who I am today. Since this is life, though, I didn't think of any of them as particularly catalytic. These catalysts began small and then grew over time into a recognizable pattern, a series of events that led me into this work. Just before I turned thirty, I examined my own thoughts, beliefs, and behaviors, trying to understand what was in my own personal baggage because my life felt like a wreck and I had no idea how to fix the wreckage and feel better.

The Beginnings

I grew up as the eldest child in a very conservative Roman Catholic family. Though my parents were very conscious of providing for my spiritual education as a Catholic, my sexual education seemed to be on an exit ramp of the "How to Get to Heaven" highway. The signposts on that highway had major sins labeled clearly, and sex was definitely one of those sins—unless it was sex that happened between heterosexual people who were married to each other and who wanted to make babies and (sometimes) express their love for each other. That kind of sex was okay as long as you didn't talk about it. However, any other sex outside those strict parameters or even wanting to think or discuss it was sinful and had to be avoided, much like those other exit ramps with their clearly labeled signs for lying, stealing, and killing.

My parents had five more children after me, so as a child I knew that babies happened when Mommy's tummy got big and then she went to the hospital. For a long time I didn't need to know more than that. When I was in third grade, I started hearing rumors of how "sex" made babies, and what "sex" actually consisted of in practice. Those secretive nuggets of information were passed along on that greatest of all mobile gossip mills: the school bus.

My mom heard from other mothers that these rumors were going around. So one night while I was washing dishes with her, she told me she had heard about the school bus conversations and wanted to make sure I had the correct information.

I wanted to die from embarrassment! We did not talk about private parts in our family unless we were in pain and had to go to the doctor. Even though my mother had always used the correct terminology—vagina and penis—to reference my and my siblings' genitals, I sure didn't want to tell her that I knew what adults did with those parts to make a baby! Surprisingly, I didn't think my information was incorrect, I just didn't want to talk about it.

For several minutes, I looked at the soapy dishwater, wishing to disappear into the floor as my mother insisted that unless I told her what I knew, she was going to tell me the details anyway. Eventually I slunk over to the counter by the wall calendar, grabbed the shopping list pad and pencil that were lying there, and wrote the following:

The man puts his umm-umm in the woman's umm-umm, and that's how the baby is made.

I could feel my face burning red-hot as I handed her the piece of paper. I remember being terrified that I would start to laugh hysterically or break down and cry. She read it over, confirmed that it was correct, and then followed with the admonition not to do it until I was married.

The end.

At no time do I recall being encouraged to think of my body and its pleasures, sexual or otherwise, as a gift from God or divine in any way. I was terrified to masturbate because I had been told it was a sin that would send you to hell. I tried touching myself twice in middle school and was so overwrought with guilt that there was no sensation of pleasure at all. In fact, I didn't "get it" with self-pleasure until I was twenty-one years old, long after I'd been engaging in sexual activity with males.

Spirituality was one side of the balance, the better side—store up your treasures in heaven, to quote the Bible—and physical pleasure would only lead the holy-seeking person away from divine love. Though I didn't want to believe that my body was evil, I realized as I sat in a therapist's office at age thirty-one that I did actually believe that I wasn't truly worthy of love and pleasure. Over the following nine months both during our sessions and in her recommended reading, I learned about those false beliefs and how my parents, my former religion, and society had told me that my body was evil, my desires were evil, and I should be guilty and ashamed for all of it. I came to realize that guilt and shame are such powerful emotions that they sap your energy to love yourself on many levels.

More Layers

Another catalyst for my work is the just-as-spotty sex education I received outside of my family. Most of my information came from friends at school and on the school bus, older siblings of friends, cousins and, like many of my 1970s peers, *Cosmopolitan* magazine. That info was juicy, gossipy, and tantalizing but ultimately not much help for someone who wasn't sexually active. Song lyrics, television shows, and movies also gave hints, but real, useful information from a source that knew more than I did and wasn't ashamed or afraid to talk about it in language I could understand was extremely rare.

There was, of course, the afternoon in fifth grade where the boys were all taken to one classroom and the girls were all taken to another where we watched filmstrips designed to give us information about puberty. I'm not sure what the boys learned... probably something to do with erections and wet dreams and body hair. In our darkened classroom, we were told about body hair, breast development, and getting your period. Topics included biological information about hormone changes and uterine lining, how to use a pad (with an elastic belt— though this was 1980, so many pads were being made with adhesive strips to stick to your panties) and a tampon. That could have been helpful, perhaps, but the filmstrip was made in the 1960s, so the drawings were weird and cartoony, more oddly funny than actually helpful. And there was very little discussion by the female teachers who were in the classroom to answer questions. Of course, most of us were far too embarrassed or confused to ask any.

In high school biology class, there was the official chapter on human reproduction as well as two weeks of health studies in ninth grade gym class. The drawings in the biology textbook were better than the filmstrip from fifth grade but still didn't look like actual people having sex, so that was still a mystery for a couple more years until I figured it out with a guy. I tried watching porn once when I was babysitting for a family that had a newfangled and gigantic satellite dish in their yard, but I was terrified that someone would find out and tell my parents.

8

and

ans

Guilt and shame were heavier motivators than curiosity when weighed in the balance of my psyche.

A later catalyst was understanding my own evolving sexuality. I was always a sensualist. I loved soft fabrics, fancy clothes that sparked my imagination, sexy lingerie, candlelight, soft whispered words, and lots of touching. In seventh grade we started changing for gym class, and suddenly I was surrounded each afternoon by seminaked girls in different stages of development. Outside the locker room, I noticed that boys' bodies were changing too. Some were getting wispy mustaches and deeper voices while some retained the look of children until high school.

I felt attractions to girls, but I knew I was supposed to like boys. Social pressure to appear heterosexual was reinforced daily by playground slurs of "You're so gay" to mean "You're stupid/weak/a jerk/not good enough." I learned to focus my burgeoning sexual energy in the "proper" place. Between ages seventeen and twenty-two, I had a lot of sex with men and it was occasionally quite fun. But I still noticed girls and women all the time.

Just before I turned twenty-two, I met a man who seemed like a very good choice for a partner. He was everything my parents had taught me was valuable in a spouse: good job, good family, attractive (but not so attractive as to be out of my league), which all added up to a definition of "stable." He was four years older than I was, and he wasn't Catholic, so I was able to maintain that I wasn't totally following my parents' programming. He was so stable that we quickly became engaged and married the following year, just weeks after my twenty-third birthday. In the course of a few years, we had two children.

From the first few months, we had some challenges sexually and interpersonally, and I had concerns about some of his manipulative behaviors. I had been honest with him from the

6

start about my feelings for women because I had a huge crush on my best friend at the time. His response was "As long as you're faithful to me, your feelings don't matter." I thought that my feelings for my friend (and attraction to women in general) would fade away and our relationship would work itself out without much intervention. I recalled that my mother had often joked that her marriage with my dad didn't get good until they'd been married ten years.

Unsurprisingly, many of our differences didn't fade or become easier. We were busy with our small children, but our incompatibilities were becoming more apparent with each passing year. I was also realizing that I was more and more attracted to women as sexual and romantic partners. In fact, I started to remember my initial attractions back in elementary and middle school and used those in enhancing my personal fantasies.

The Healing Journey

That makes it sound easy and effortless, doesn't it? Yet I, like most human beings, was a great avoider of painful reality. I had spent years stuffing my uncomfortable feelings into a small spot somewhere inside. If I didn't look at them, then they weren't real, right? So why did I keep thinking about these "unreal" feelings?

There is an old saying: If you always do what you've always done, you'll always get what you've always got.

I wanted something different. I wanted to be happy and content in my life. By the time I was twenty-nine and my daughters were four and two, I was miserable. I wanted to get rid of the ache in my stomach and the tension in my shoulders and lower back that were part of every day. I wanted to wake up and have everything that was wrong in my life and my marriage changed into the way things should have been. However, it was pretty difficult to make changes in my life when I wasn't willing to be honest with myself.

I spent so long denying what I was feeling emotionally that I developed physical symptoms of ill health. My lower back started hurting so badly I couldn't bend over to tie my shoes even when sitting down. The ache in my stomach became severe acid reflux, and I had to eliminate many foods from my diet until I could determine that I had become lactose intolerant —and that lasted for a year. I was snappy and irritable with my children and my husband. I wanted to cry all the time. I felt like I was dying inside, that my outer body was just a shell that wore clothes and talked to people on its own, but that no one knew the real me.

Initially my husband would not agree to try therapy. I called a therapist and asked for a recommendation for a book for us to read. The book he recommended was *Conscious Loving: The Journey to Co-Commitment* by Gay and Kathlyn Hendricks. My husband and I started reading it together and did a few exercises, but without someone to help us, we ended up even more frustrated and tense. It was months later that he agreed to try couples' counseling with the counselor who had suggested the book.

After three mostly unproductive sessions, the counselor proposed that he work with my husband one-on-one for a while, and then we'd try again. I was waking up to my own need for healing, not as a wife but as a woman.

I was thirty-one years old. It was time to *get real*. I found an amazing therapist for myself. Her skill, presence, and wisdom combined into another catalyst, revealing to me my own calling to bear witness to another person's journey of self-recovery as a counselor and minister. I was amazed by the powerful safety she offered me simply by sitting and listening and stating her observations.

I began to open up to myself as never before. In order to

unpack my sexual baggage and grow into a holistic version of myself, I had to get honest about who I was at that point and how I had let myself go into hiding. It took a few months before I noticed I was feeling better. I started swimming at the YMCA to help my back, and I became very aware of what foods I was eating. I would see this same therapist off and on for the next five years. A few years after that, as I was starting my own counseling practice, she sent me referrals—a sure sign of confidence in the value of my approach.

I continued to reclaim my feminine spirit through music, meditation, reading inspiring books, and learning about sex in a positive, nonjudgmental way. I finally believed I was important enough to listen to. And what my heart was saying was: You are not meant for this marriage; you and your children deserve a better atmosphere at home.

My husband and I separated in early 2004 after ten years of marriage, and I came out of the closet as a lesbian. Even though I was still working on my baggage, I was able to reclaim my joy in many areas of my life. I wasn't trying to pretend I was someone else: a copy of my mother, June Cleaver, some mythological perfect wife and mother, a straight woman. I determined that in the years ahead I would parent my children differently. I would teach them positive attitudes about their bodies, about love, and about the ups and downs of relationships. Not trying to fit into a box made by someone else allowed me to reclaim those parts of me that I had cut off (or been forced to cut off) in order to fit into the box labeled "Appropriate Woman."

Over the next few years, I worked several part-time jobs while completing my bachelor's degree in psychology and doing research on sex positivity. I read lots of books, looked online for solid information from reputable sex-positive sources like Babeland (formerly Toys in Babeland) and Good Vibrations, where shoppers for sex toys and erotica were treated with respect and were encouraged and expected to ask questions and where information about safer sex practices, BDSM, and "alternative sexuality" was openly available. I followed the blogs of sexperts like Tristan Taormino, Dr. Patti Britton, and Em and Lo.

When I finished my degree in December 2008 at the ripe age of thirty-seven, I thought about continuing my education to become a licensed sex therapist. But there was one more catalyst. In a conversation with a longtime friend, she mentioned that she was considering enrolling in a seminary to become ordained and to practice as a spiritual counselor. I sensed all the catalysts line up together, and I knew that I was being called to that too.

During my years as an undergrad, I continued to unpack my sexual and spiritual luggage and talk with others. I had noticed recurring themes in those conversations: assumptions; religious taboos, restrictions, and shame; self-esteem and performance anxiety; difficulty with sexual conversations and desires; questions about pain and sexual violence and a fairly large bag full of trust issues. The more I unpacked and worked on healing those areas for myself, the more frequently I seemed to have conversations with others about just those topics. I realized people were hungry to talk about sex in a non-shaming, exciting, affirming and, yes, spiritual way.

During the years I was finishing my degree in spiritual counseling, I started my own business as a sex coach. My clients were women and men; young, middle-aged, and senior citizens; gay, lesbian, bisexual, and hetero. I worked with people who were exploring new territory, digging deep into their past behaviors and patterns, seeking greater knowledge of themselves and deeper connections with their partners. I always brought the awareness of a client's spiritual self and spiritual growth into the sessions. Part of the work was encouraging each person to integrate sex and spirit into their embodied self and release the sense of shame that often accompanied their desires.

Where Am I Now?

Since that time, I've learned much more about spiritual sexuality and continued to examine my own beliefs and behaviors, especially as lovers and friends have come into my life and given me new perspectives of myself. I've learned that my mismatched luggage is actually an attractively quirky set of experiences and knowledge that I can share with others because I'm no longer scared of what's inside. I've created a spiritually rich life filled with joy, yummy sex, and peace with my past. A few years ago I met a woman who shared my desires for deep intimacy, honest communication, and enthusiastic sex. We married in 2017.

My daughters are now young adults, and they had all the information they could handle (and maybe more than they wanted to hear from their mom!) throughout their childhood. They are the ones their friends turned to in their teen years for accurate information and support. No more turning to *Cosmo* for advice. They are finding their individual paths in relationships, work, and as spiritual sexual women. I love that we are close and continue to have conversations about who they are and who they want to be.

That is why I am called to this work. I want to help others just like you to unpack their sexual baggage and find the wonderful spirit of *self* inside every labeled box or bag. By reclaiming my mismatched luggage, I found that my body's truth was much easier to identify and own. I want that for you too.

Know this: there is nothing inherently wrong with you.

You were created with desires for connections of body, mind, and soul. Your work as a divinely human being is to continue to remember that you are a fully embodied spirit, and the path to spiritual connection most often happens not outside the body on some ethereal plane but by living fully within and through your beautiful, capable, desirable body.

QUESTIONS FOR REFLECTION

What are some pieces that fill your mismatched luggage?

Do you have some ideas of what pieces you want to keep and which ones you can release?

What do you think and feel when you read the phrase "spiritual sexual self"?

2

THE PASSPORT:

EMBODIMENT IS IDENTITY

Embodiment is the practice of attending to your sensations.
—Dr. Arielle Schwartz

EMBODIMENT CAN SEEM A BIT CONFUSING BECAUSE IT IS DEFINED as a visible form of an intangible idea, quality, or feeling. For example: "She was the embodiment of grace and style." Embodiment in this sense relies on the hearer or reader understanding the idea or quality that is being described. That is not precisely what I mean when I use this term. I could more accurately say "anthropological embodiment," which is a way of describing bodily experiences and understanding what it means to live with awareness of your body both internally and as you interact with the world around you.

In somatic psychology, the principle of embodiment says that everything we experience is stored in the body and mind, whether we think we can remember something or not. Similarly, dream psychologists posit that every face we see in our dreams are faces that we have seen in our waking life even if we did not interact with that person. Being able to remember previous experiences in our bodies helps us to react to stimuli in ways that help to keep us safe, such as backing away from the street corner instead of stepping out to cross the street when we hear a large vehicle coming our way.

Embodiment also involves our innate human capacity to learn about and adapt to our ever-changing environment. This capacity for learning and adapting is wrapped within and around paying attention to what it feels like to be alive in our bodies. We understand that the sensations of digestion or indigestion, pain in our joints or muscles, hunger, heart palpitations, or having to urinate are part of the package deal with having a body. Yet a body is so much more than simply sensations. We have a mind inside our body that helps to separate and explain the sensations; this mind works to help us understand emotions that we learn to associate with certain sensations, such as tension in the jaw muscles that can be an indicator of feeling angry.

Physical embodiment integrates three sensory-feedback systems—exteroception, proprioception, and interoception. I learned these terms while studying the work of Peter Levine, whose breakthrough book, *Waking the Tiger, Healing Trauma*, changed the psychological approach to trauma therapy in 1997, though he had been refining his methods since the late 1970s. While these may be new words for you, I think you'll find you already understand their explanations very well.

- **Exteroception** refers to the sensory experience of the external environment through sensory neurons that travel from the periphery of the body (eyes, ears, nose, tongue, skin) to the brain (sights, sounds, touch sensations, etc.).

- **Proprioception** is the sensory feedback about the location of the body in space. This awareness includes positioning and balance.

- **Interoception** involves the sensory experience inside the body. This can include hunger, thirst, sleepiness, body temperature, and pain. Interoception's information about our muscles and organs can lead us to understand emotional reactions, such as "butterflies in the stomach" often labeled as fear or anxiety.

These feedback systems create a felt sense of self. You know you are alive because you can feel air on your skin, you feel your legs moving as you walk on the sidewalk, and you feel hungry and you can have thoughts about those sensations.

Some of those physical sensations can be dulled or nonexistent due to physical injury or damage. We can also learn to shut down our awareness of sensation as a response to trauma. Using somatic psychology, embodiment can be enhanced through mindfulness practices such as focusing on breathing to calm down or doing a body scan to note areas of tension. Listening to and understanding body messages become core elements of healing when we embrace embodiment. Even if we are physically inhibited from sensation, we can develop the capacity to "feel" all the way to our edges, to understand how to fully inhabit our bodies without numbing out.

This may sound a little esoteric, or even unlikely. Here is an example of what I mean. A woman I knew several years ago was dating a man with a spinal cord injury. His body was paralyzed below his ribs, which meant that he not only was unable to move, he had no ability to feel touch, temperature, or pain in his legs, hips, buttocks, or genitals. He also had difficulty with digestion and elimination of feces due to his spinal nerve damage.

When they decided to become sexual, he was adept at arousal and stimulation of her vulva, clitoris, and vagina with his hands and with oral stimulation. However, because of his injury, he was unable to achieve or maintain an erection for intercourse. His doctor prescribed an injectable vasodilator that served the same purpose as an oral vasodilator, such as Viagra, that allows the blood vessels of the penis to expand and hold blood so the penis can become erect enough to be inserted into a vagina or anus.

While this was a wonderful addition to their sex life, both my friend and her boyfriend wanted a deeper connection. They started practicing meditation and guided imagery together before and during sex to enhance his ability to connect with the part of his body that was unable to receive sensory feedback through exteroception. Over time, he reported that he was able to use his internal sense of arousal (interoception) and focus that in his genitals. This focus on his embodiment brought greater joy to their sexual experiences because he now felt more fully present during intercourse.

When Trauma Gets Embodied

Even if you would not describe yourself as having a history of trauma, many of us in this culture have been taught to ignore our body's messages. We diet to lose weight and tell ourselves we're not hungry, or we dull the hunger with substances like amphetamines in various forms to trick ourselves into believing that our bodies are mistaken. We play a sport and hurt an ankle, but we pretend that the pain is not significant so we can stay in the game. We slip and fall on the ice while walking in a parking lot, but we pretend that the cuts on our hands don't bother us because we're embarrassed about losing our balance.

I've done all those things, and at times, society has lauded me for being disciplined, stoic, and brave. The reward is greater for people who are paid to have their bodies perform and present with near perfection: athletes, stunt people, models, and actors. These people are often pushed to be simultaneously hyperaware of their bodies and the impact their appearance or performance has on others while ignoring the sensations of their bodies for rest, nourishment, and medical attention.

When we experience trauma through abuse, especially prolonged abuse over time, the danger that we experience outside our bodies (verbal, emotional, mental, etc.) or the danger that is inflicted upon us (physical and sexual) can increase our ability to ignore our bodies because we are focused on the real fear of the greater danger from someone else. Ignoring or "checking out" of a frightening or painful experience, also known as dissociation, at the time it is happening, and with the spiritual and psychological pain of being abused, can show up in physical pains later that seem unrelated to the situation at hand. An example of this is the digestive problem I talked about having in the first chapter that developed after several years of conflict and discomfort in my first marriage.

Delayed physical response can show up as muscle tension or spasms, diarrhea, or heart arrhythmia when we think the danger has passed, or even years later. Multiple studies published in the *Journal of American Medicine* have linked post-traumatic stress disorder (PTSD) with autoimmune diseases. Our bodies know what we've experienced, and if our minds and souls are left unhealed, the damage can be ongoing. Seeking a counselor whom you trust is key to helping unravel and heal these wounds while also addressing the physical needs of your body through medical treatments and other therapeutic methods.

Things don't have to get to the point of severe pain or illness before you deal with them though. You can start right now to address any places of disconnection. Most of us have learned to diminish our awareness of sensation or pain, even as we want to seek healing and integration. Have you ever woken up after a nap and were unsure if you had been sleeping for twenty minutes or two hours? Beginning to wake up to ourselves can sometimes feel exactly like waking up after a deep sleep. We are confused and disoriented, and sensations can come in and out of focus.

Calming Anxiety and Increasing Focus

The first step seems almost too easy, yet I promise you the results can be profound. This first step to becoming more embodied is simply to tune into your breathing. You can focus on your breathing, listening to your inhale and your exhale, noting if you are breathing shallowly in your chest or deeply into your diaphragm at any time. Inhaling for a count of five and then exhaling for a count of ten activates the vagus nerve and can shift your mental state from anxiety and chaos to calm and centered.

Practice this focus with a gentleness and sense of ease. You don't have to make this one more thing on your to-do list that must be checked off. Instead, you can invite your breath to become a source of renewal and revitalization.

Once you are in a state of calm, it is far easier to remember how to feel yourself all the way to your edges. You can then use your senses to bring you fully present.

- Identify five sounds you hear.
- Name the items you can see around you.
- Note the odors in the air.
- Touch the fabric of your clothes and the surfaces nearest you with your fingers.
- Generate saliva and swallow, feeling the muscular actions of your mouth and throat.

With continued awareness, you will more often remember where your body is located in space and avoid some distractions that lead to stubbed toes and banged elbows. Most importantly, the more you embrace your embodiment, the better you'll be able to show up for yourself in the realm of unpacking those bags that have been weighing you down and preventing you from fully engaging in your life and your spiritual journey.

Body Scan and Centering Practice for Expanded Embodiment

I developed this practice using a combination of yoga nidra and guided meditation techniques as a way to help my clients become centered at the beginning of a session that focuses on deep wounds. It is a bit lengthy to begin, but as you become more adept at this, you'll probably devise your own shortcuts that allow you to become centered in just a few breaths. I do recommend taking longer times for centering several times a week because it is so good for your body, mind, and spirit to slow down and bring your energies back into yourself to remember who you are as a soul so that you can refocus on the outside world from a more embodied place.

Read this through a few times before you practice it so that you have the sequence down and won't have to come out of the practice to read the next steps.

Preparation and Breathing

1) Find a quiet space where you can sit or lie down for fifteen to twenty minutes.

2) Settle yourself in and fine tune your comfort level to the best of your ability. Get a blanket or shawl to keep you warm, but not so warm that you'll fall asleep (though you might get so

relaxed you fall asleep anyway). Arrange your body so that you can focus on the awareness within you.

3) Close your eyes or simply soften your gaze with eyes open to allow for your focus to be internal.

4) Inhale gently for a count of five, and hold your breath for a count of four.

5) Exhale slowly to a count of ten. Repeat this until you feel your body release whatever tension you have.

Integrating the Body

1) Focus your awareness on your right thumb, breathing easily and feeling into the space your thumb occupies.

2) Move your awareness across the right hand. At each shift of awareness, note how you sense the focus of your mind.

3) Move your awareness farther to the palm of the right hand, back of the hand, wrist, arm, shoulder, right side waist, hip, leg, foot, and each toe, starting at your big toe and ending with your little toe.

4) Shift your awareness to your left thumb, and move your awareness along the same path on the left as you did on the right.

5) Now become aware of the rest of your body: your head, face, neck, and torso. Feel the entire right side of your body, then the left side of your body, the front and then the back. Finally, focus on your entire body all at once. Keep breathing.

Reaching Out to the Earth

Once you are integrated in your body, focus on the bottoms of your feet and imagine that you are sending small roots down through the floor (or however many floors there are between you and the ground) and into the earth. Allow the roots to burrow into the earth of your imagination and bring up the energy of the earth as you also breathe and release anything you wish into the ground. Stay here for several breaths and then imagine saying "thank you" to the earth and bringing your roots back up into your body.

Take a few final breaths, and bring yourself into the present by wiggling your fingers and toes and giving your body a lovely stretch and a smile.

Penny's Story

Penny came to me after attending a presentation I gave on embodiment and pleasure. She was interested in learning why she rarely achieved orgasm and how she could stop feeling guilty for disappointing her husband of three years. Both partners were in their late twenties and had been sexually active in previous relationships before getting together.

Penny described herself as a woman who was uncomfortable being naked in front of anyone, even her husband. She came from a middle-class family and reported that she had not experienced physical or sexual trauma. We began with exercises to help Penny tune into herself, to find her inner voice of desire and pleasure for her own sake, not just as a function of her husband's wishes. She practiced being naked and viewing herself in a mirror at home.

We met every other week for several months, and within three sessions, Penny had begun to explore what it meant for her to feel pleasure in touching herself in sensual, nonsexual ways. I suggested she begin with taking warm baths, setting a calm and inviting atmosphere for herself with soft lighting and music to help her focus on her enjoyment and not what her husband was doing or thinking elsewhere in the house. While in the bath, she was to take time to feel the warmth and softness of the water, to allow herself to relax, and afterward I encouraged her to speak positive affirmations to herself while applying lotion.

During our counseling sessions, Penny talked about her feeling that all her lovers had been rushing to get through foreplay and directly to intercourse. Rarely had she felt urgent desire for a partner because by the time she was starting to get truly aroused, her male partner had already finished his orgasm and was either ready to be done or was rushing her to achieve an orgasm that she wasn't ready to experience. Penny said that she felt frustrated, angry, and sad with herself that she wasn't able to easily reach orgasm and was ready to call off her search for pleasure. She had occasionally given herself an orgasm through self-pleasure, but she discounted those as "not real orgasms."

Some of Penny's challenges involved not feeling in control of her own body and thinking that her body was supposed to be available and ready for sex whenever her husband was aroused. Together we discussed the female cycle of sexual arousal and the time it took for the average woman to reach peak arousal and orgasm. Penny realized that she had been rushed by her lovers and by her ideas of what she should be feeling and experiencing. This stopped her from truly being present with what her body was actually sensing and wanting.

Further homework for Penny involved talking with her husband about slowing down, focusing for several weeks on refraining from sexual interaction and instead using the Sensate Focus exercises (originally developed by sex researchers Masters and Johnson in the 1950s) to learn sensual, nonsexual touch, how to ask for more of what she enjoyed, and to ask for touch that was irritating or unpleasant to change or stop. She reported that his initial reluctance to slow down was replaced with enjoyment of the process and led to increased physical and verbal affection throughout the day.

After four weeks of no sexual contact, Penny was excited to start exploring intercourse again. At our next session, she told me that although she had not reached orgasm during intercourse, her husband continued to touch her and stimulate her with his hand after his own orgasm. She didn't feel rushed, and she was able to experience orgasm.

Penny continued to expand her awareness and experience in staying present in her body, self-pleasure through sensuality, affirmations, and masturbation, and asking for more touch from her husband. She journaled about her insights and talked openly with me about her thoughts regarding her parents' admonitions about expectations of female modesty and speaking up. She realized that she had focused so diligently on being what she thought her husband wanted that she had missed out on her own capacity for desire and pleasure. She left our last session excited to keep exploring staying present with herself and feeling all her sensations.

QUESTIONS FOR REFLECTION

What does "embodiment" bring up for you?

How did it feel to practice the body scan described above?

When do you feel most out of touch with your body versus when you feel most alive in your skin?

3

THE TRAVEL SET:

OWNING YOUR BAGGAGE

Simplicity is making the journey of this life with just baggage enough.
—Charles Dudley Warner

BY THE TIME WE REACH ADULTHOOD, WE HAVE BAGGAGE. IT'S NOT necessarily a bad thing to have. We learn through trial and error, as well as words of teaching and admonishment, what people expect of us and how we want to interact with them from our early years. We come to each new relationship with our memories of the past and our mental models of who we are and what others will do based on our experiences. Yet if we want to continue on our path to healing and wholeness, we arrive at a time when we need to unpack our bags, claim what is ours, and decide what is needed for the journey ahead. We must do this again and again as life goes on.

Baggage is a fairly common term in therapy and counseling. It has made its way into our cultural lingo as well. We often hear people talk about themselves or others as having "lots of baggage" or "too much baggage" to be in a relationship. Because it is a commonplace term, there are many ways to interpret "baggage." However, I have created the following definition for my work:

Baggage: a set of beliefs, assumptions, experiences, and behaviors that allow us to feel safe, survive adversity or trauma, and make a personal structure for functioning in our past lives but which can come to feel cumbersome and limiting in our current lives.

Unless we learn to unpack our baggage and own our lessons, mistakes, and assumptions, we will be caught in repetitive patterns that prevent true intimacy. Instead of saying "intimacy," think of "into me see." We want to be seen, accepted, and loved for who we really are. In order for intimacy to happen with others, it first has to happen with ourselves. Even with our fears of intimacy and vulnerability, I believe it's what we all want. We have to know and accept ourselves deeply so that we can love ourselves as the embodied souls we are. When we know deep love of self we gain insight into how we want to be loved by others. We can then set healthy boundaries for ourselves and also give concrete information and examples to our partners.

Oftentimes this need for unpacking our baggage comes when we begin or end a relationship. There is nothing like the mirror of another person to show us all our foibles and perceived inadequacies. Mirrors are a part of all our relationships with friends, work colleagues, children, and people we know through our social networks, but since we are here to unpack our sexual baggage, we'll focus on sexual relationships now.

Jiddu Krishnamurti (1895-1986) was an Indian philosopher who authored several books and spoke widely about personal growth and human relationships. He was one of the first to identify relationships as mirrors of the personal psyche. He said:

"Relationship is the mirror in which we see ourselves as we are."

"All life is a movement in relationship."

Have you started dating someone new only to discover that they sounded or acted much like a previous lover with whom you had difficulties? Have you had friends or family notice that you have a "type" that you tend to date? Do you have similar conversations or arguments with people from different parts of your life? These are the mirror relationships that Krishnamurti noted.

When we see ourselves through another person's view, it can be a bit jarring. It's not always easy to look at our own baggage. The things we carry are often shoved away out of plain sight. Courage and compassion are the watchwords for unpacking those bags. It can be helpful to have a sense of what you might be getting into before you dive in.

Baggage Labels

One—or several—of the bags that we carry around with us could be labeled FAMILY EXPECTATIONS or CULTURAL EXPECTATIONS. Many of us were raised in families in which we had spoken or unspoken expectations about how we should behave based on our sex. Girls were encouraged and expected to be helpful, kind, meek, agreeable, prim, quiet, friendly, and only interested in sex or dating as a way to get to the prize of landing a suitable husband. Boys were encouraged and expected to be rough-and-tumble, loud, athletic, financially and mechanically savvy, and always interested in sex without wanting to be tied to a commitment. Of course, these descriptions limit our options of full human expression, but perhaps you recognize one or two of the expectations in the list that rings true for your family or culture. It is often the case that the society reinforces these family expectations or vice versa with family members reinforcing the cultural dictates.

When looking through these bags of expectations, you might feel angry that no one let you choose how you wanted to be.

Expectations can help us rise to a certain level of competence, but they don't often allow us to be fully human in all our complexity. The good news is that you can make a choice now about the way you wish to live into your human potential. You can learn new job skills; try out clothing options and body decoration like jewelry, cosmetics, or tattoos; become a better communicator; explore a sport or hobby; and dive deeply into your spiritual sexual self and throw off the confines of gender stereotypes. Women can be far more than what culture tells us to be, and men can as well. Don't give in to the lure of limits to what you can express and wear and pursue because of some "gender norms." We are far richer as individuals and as a society when all people own and express themselves outside rigid stereotypes that are often used to oppress and repress our full humanity.

Another bag might carry the label PAIN. It can be terrifying to look at our pain because every being from one-celled amoebae to the flowers in our garden to other mammals is designed to seek pleasure and avoid pain. However pain is part of the experience of living, so we are going to come up against painful experiences throughout our lives. The baggage of pain happens when we are not able to express the pain as it is happening or when the pain recurs so often and to such a degree that it becomes trauma.

As an example, most of us have stubbed our toes hundreds of times in our lives. Do you remember every single time you stubbed a toe? Probably not. You may remember a few instances based on the severity of the pain or the uniqueness of the situation, but most of the time you stub your toe, you let out a yell, maybe say a few choice curse words, and then go on with your day. You don't think about the toe stubbing until you're recounting the story or you stub your toe again.

When pain happens that we don't express such as being bullied and threatened with harm if we "tattle" or when we are repeatedly abused and told to cover it up, that pain becomes part of our baggage, the part we don't often look at but which silently guides our actions. That's when pain becomes trauma and we diminish our expression of self and living to avoid dealing with it. We may tell ourselves that "It's too hard/too scary/not important/happened a long time ago/isn't relevant now, etc." However, the longer the trauma goes unexpressed and unexamined, the heavier it becomes and the more that trauma will live in your subconscious and silently direct your life. I talked about trauma in the last chapter, and it will come up again later. Know that unpacking the baggage of trauma can be far less frightening when enlisting the help of a counselor.

Some other labels that you may have on your baggage could include: ASSUMPTIONS, PERFORMANCE, BODY IMAGE, FEELING WORTHY, and RELIGIOUS TABOOS about sex. Most of us have bags like this to a greater or lesser degree. Even those people you look up to often have baggage. We are all far more alike than we are different. If you've noticed how heavy your bags have become, how you may be repeating the same thought patterns and behaviors that you bring to your relationships, and experiencing the same frustrating results, now is as good a time as any to dive deeper into those bags and see what wisdom is waiting there for you among the labels.

RANIA'S STORY

Rania was a forty-three-year-old woman who came to me to work on communication issues with her husband. She claimed that she wanted to open up to him in a deeper way and create more intimacy. She said that she felt like a cardboard cut-out of a person sometimes because she repeatedly said she was "fine" when she actually wasn't.

Throughout our initial conversations, I noticed that she seemed to shy away from saying anything negative about her husband. She repeatedly made remarks about herself and their children, but when I asked about ways that he irritated her or times when she was angry with him, she would launch into another story of how she didn't feel she could talk to him. I pointed this out to her, and she agreed to think about it before our next session.

In following sessions, Rania opened up to me and to herself about how very angry she was with the way her husband treated her. She felt her husband didn't appreciate her intelligence and only responded to her in ways that made her question her perceptions. She said that during conflicts, he would go over explanations repeatedly using the same words rather than trying to create dialogue to learn more about what she was trying to understand. She admitted that she often downplayed her skills and intelligence in order to get him to talk to her more.

As I questioned her about this, she recalled that it was a pattern in all her sexual relationships. She would start out strong and confident, but within a few weeks or months, she recalled deferring to her male lovers or boyfriends in areas ranging from where to go for dinner, how many layers to wear on an outdoor hike, or whether or not to buy new appliances. She also noted that her mother behaved this way with her father prior to their divorce when Rania was fourteen. Rania's mother became more confident after the divorce and was able to make decisions for the household, but Rania's perception was that her mother was unable to keep a man since she only went on a few dates during Rania's remaining high school years.

Our sessions were then able to focus on what keeping a man around meant to Rania based on her experiences as a child and how that pattern showed up in her adult relationships. We talked about what her children were perceiving about women's roles and what the impact of that might be on them. Rania was able to start examining her own baggage around empowerment, the roles of husband and wife—which she discovered were not the roles that she wanted to live out in her relationship—along with the anger she was carrying about her parents' divorce and the sadness she felt for her mother.

Over the next few months, Rania was able to define for herself what she truly wanted, and she began to talk to her husband more frankly about what she was learning relating to her needs and her feelings. Though she was initially nervous asking for change, she found that as she opened up, her husband was able to talk of his childhood memories of his parents and their style of interaction. Both of them realized that they had been unconsciously re-creating their childhood impressions of marriage, and that in order to grow into their own relationship, they had more work to do in both self-discovery and in sharing their inner experiences and memories with each other.

Owning the baggage that was dragging her down allowed Rania to look at it with a clearer set of eyes and to decide what was worth taking with her in her life's journey. As we neared the end of our months of work, Rania remarked that she was learning more about her husband as a person and that they were communicating better and more equally than ever before.

QUESTIONS FOR REFLECTION

How does your baggage show up?

How do you know if your baggage is limiting you?

What do you notice with a partner when you're being held back or stuck from dragging around your unexamined baggage?

4

THE STEAMER TRUNK:

EXPERIENCES OF PAIN DON'T HAVE TO RUN YOUR LIFE

Pain is inevitable. Suffering is optional.
—*Haruki Murakami*

DISCOMFORT IS PART OF LIFE. EVEN THE MOST CUSHIONED AND well-loved child has to learn to walk, and that involves falling. We live with our fears, our jealousies, and our disappointments from unmet expectations. We may have trauma from other people's words and deeds or from our reactions and stories we created about the intentions behind those words and deeds. Pain and discomfort are part of being human, and it is human tendency to bring those experiences and subsequent scars with us into our current reality and relationships.

We may not realize that we're doing it. We may think, especially at the beginning, that this new relationship isn't anything like the old one (or the past several). How many times, though, have you or someone you know said some version of the following statement: Why do I keep dating/having a relationship with the same person who is wearing a different face?

It's very common to begin dating someone new only to

realize that the issues we face with a current partner are ones we have faced in previous relationships, often all the way back to our family of origin. One of the therapeutic styles that addresses this directly is Imago Relationship Therapy (IRT). In 1988, Dr. Harville Hendrix wrote a book describing his work as the developer of IRT (sometimes called Imago Therapy). This book was entitled *Getting the Love You Want: A Guide for Couples* and has been a best seller ever since.

The crux of this approach is to help people recognize that there is often a mirror or connection between the frustrations and struggles we experience in our adult relationships and our early childhood relationships with parents and other primary caregivers. For example, if you are a person who experienced lots of criticism and judgment in your childhood, you may often feel similar criticism and disapproval coming from your partner. You may also notice fears of abandonment or smothering in your relationship if those were something you experienced in your family.

While we may attempt to cope with some of these issues, we won't see them end until we've explored and healed these feelings and wounds and can tell our partners about them. It's quite common we find that our partners are playing out their own childhood issues with us as the foil/parent figure. You might have heard it said that we marry our parents, and this is often how it shows up.

You might think it would be an easy thing to see. Imagine coming home at seven thirty on a Thursday night when you're usually home by six. Your wife says, "Gee, you're home late. I thought you'd be home in time for dinner." You hear that comment as criticism for working too much or not taking care of your part of the housework. The comment reminds you of the times when your mother embarrassed you in front of your friends about not being able to go out because you hadn't finished your chores. You note your reaction and the memory and tell your wife about it and ask her if she is angry about your delay and is trying to let you know about her feelings by using a seemingly neutral comment. She responds by telling you her own feelings and thoughts, and you have a calm and caring discussion about expectations and emotions.

Sounds like a healthy interaction, doesn't it? Unfortunately, most of us don't get a foundation in understanding and using relationship skills that would lead to this type of interaction until *after* we've gone several rounds along the cycle of anger, blame, attack, stonewall, pain, and resentment, as well as the demise of a few relationships.

There are also occasions in which the event or action that one person experiences as painful or that triggers a memory of previous trauma is not perceived by their partner as something scary, dangerous, or aggressive. There is a saying from the world of twelve-step programs: *If I'm hysterical, it's historical.* When the response to an issue seems out of proportion to the act, it is time to look deeper and find out where the root of the problem lies.

I do **not** mean that anyone needs to stay in an abusive situation or be treated badly in order to work through your baggage.

What I advocate is sitting within the container of relationship where both people are doing their best to be conscious and open to doing the work of healing. In this container we can find the strength and courage to become vulnerable and honest about our fears and our patterns of sabotage. We can learn to be patient with the process of uncovering the original pain and the subsequent layers of pain or protective behaviors that are related to the primary hurt. We can practice calming and centering ourselves so that we are able to listen to our partner talk about their pain without trying to justify our actions, minimize their response, or slap a quick fix on the discomfort. We also practice stating our own hurts and fears without blaming, shaming, or using other methods to turn away from the discomfort we feel.

Changing the Story

How do we shift our focus so that experiences of pain aren't having undue influence on our current or future responses? How can we stop our memories from keeping us so vigilant against further pain that we avoid intimacy by any means necessary?

We do this by forming new neural pathways in our brains. These new pathways are the results of changing our thoughts and our behaviors and of building novel habits of response to familiar situations. The human brain is incredibly malleable—but humans are also inherently lazy. We want the easy payoff, the quick fix, the fastest route, the magic pill. That's what makes changing so difficult. Once those fast and easy paths are in place, it takes consciousness and determination to change the patterns. But it can be done!

Neural plasticity has evolved as the study of the malleable nature of the brain. Rewiring your brain is a dynamic process that happens within the relationship of your mind, brain, and body. Researcher Michael Merzenich says in the book *The Brain that Changes Itself*, that practicing a new habit under the right conditions can change hundreds of millions and possibly billions of the connections between the nerve cells in our neural pathways.

To use an image that many of us know, I invite you to think about a trail in the woods. Some trails are faint because they don't get a lot of use. The more a trail gets used by people, the flatter, wider, and easier to traverse it becomes. Similarly, as you focus on thoughts, feelings, and actions over and over again, you make neural pathways in your brain that become easier and easier to use, often without realizing how unconscious those habits have become.

That's what makes changing your mind and rewiring your brain so exciting. Notice I didn't say easy! You get to challenge yourself to stop using the pathways that don't make you feel good and create new pathways to encourage thoughts, feelings, and behaviors that enhance your enjoyment of life. You can build on your ability to stay grounded and calm in the face of scary things like confrontation or criticism. You can also learn to stop beating yourself up for perceived failings and accept yourself as the complex, ever-growing person that you are.

Here are some real-life examples of the ways we get stuck in the comfortable "velvet rut" of old pathways—those behaviors that become so habitual we don't realize how restrictive they can be. Some are not harmful, just examples of repetition, but some can become harmful to our health and happiness.

- You drive, bike, or walk to your workplace along the same streets every day even though there are multiple ways to get there.
- You go to your favorite restaurant and order the same thing (or one of three same things) even though there are many items on the menu.
- You tell your friends that you want to get in better shape, to start exercising, but at the end of the day, you get home from work and sit down to a couple of beers and three hours of video games.
- You get angry with your boss, and instead of talking with her about it, you complain to a coworker and make plans to go out after work, and the next day you are sullen and detached in the office.
- You go out on a date with a new person, and before the first half hour is up you're already telling yourself

> how many ways this person is not right for you, just
> like the last one and the one before that.

- Your spouse says something that hurts your feelings,
  and you react by leaving the room, turning on the TV,
  and ignoring everyone in the house for the rest of the
  evening.

Why does this happen?

It happens because what most of us have learned to do is to hide our pain from others and sometimes from ourselves. We create easy-to-wear masks that show others who we think they need or want us to be. Yet that pain, if left unexamined, unhealed, can become the puppeteer running our lives. When we understand why we do things, we can work on specific ways to counteract the behaviors that hold us back.

Sometimes these ways of hiding pain are subtle: staying busy so that we don't have quiet time to feel lonely or scared, or focusing on our work or kids and the rewards that come with being a "good employee" or "great parent." No one can fault us for those things, right? Some behaviors, like drinking or gambling, can start out as fun diversions that can take us from being sociable to being belligerent or anxious from the stress of having to wear these masks.

All these behaviors can create a wall between us and the people with whom we'd like to be close. Often we let our guard down long enough to enter into a relationship, but at the first sign of conflict, we start the process of defending, pushing away, retreating into ourselves, reverting to the practices that we have perfected in the past. Ostensibly, this is for our own protection, but what happens when pain is running the show is that we have trouble discerning the difference between a misunderstanding or miscommunication and deliberate harm.

You might have heard of the term codependency to describe a relationship in which one person takes care of another person, mentally, emotionally, and/or physically, and neglects to take care of themselves. This is often a result of past pain, past training—for both people—running the relationship. This is common, though not exclusive, to people coming from families where addiction or mental illness was present in one or both parents or in the entire family system.

What does this codependent behavior look like on a day-to-day level?

Person A has learned that to take responsibility for their own thoughts, behaviors, and feelings is painful and difficult and so they allow someone else to do those things... and then they get resentful and angry. Sometimes they have an addiction, but not always.

Person B has learned to be responsible for taking care of others by anticipating and managing difficult behaviors, making excuses for them, covering their tracks of misdeeds, or actively enabling an addiction while also ignoring, downplaying, or denying their own wants, needs, boundaries, and reactions to avoid facing their own pain... and then they get resentful and angry.

This is far more common than we like to think because most of us were raised in a codependent culture in which it is expected that certain people will take care of others and not ask for much in return while others will be the "dysfunctional one" in the relationship. This has less to do with the sex of the partners and more to do with the family culture in which each partner was raised. Some families teach males to be strong and make all the decisions while females are to be agreeable and keep the household running. Other families allow males to act as unreliable adolescents and teach females that all the work of strength and action comes down to them.

It's easy to get wrapped up in "the way it's always been" and not take the initiative—and the risk of rejection—to change an uncomfortable situation or relationship. Yet if we want to unpack this trunk and travel more lightly on life's journey, this is often our biggest area of growth and one that will impact our efforts to unpack other bags.

Sexual Trauma: Rape, Incest, Sexual Abuse, and Harassment

Hundreds of books and articles have been written about the effects of sexual trauma. I cannot begin to cover in this book all the ways in which sexual trauma, especially if left unexamined and unhealed, can affect your sexual expression and all your relationships. If you are a person who has experienced sexual trauma, please seek the help of a counselor who works with sexual trauma to address the hurt and find ways to heal.

Many of us have histories of trauma, and we can learn how to accept and love ourselves back into wholeness, but it is often more difficult to do this without therapeutic assistance. Talking about our trauma can help us to feel less alone and more empowered to do the work of healing. Don't be afraid to interview several therapists or counselors to find the one who fits you best.

In a previous chapter I talked about trauma that becomes stuck in the body. This is often the result of not expressing and releasing the effects of the painful or shocking experience. Sometimes this stuckness shows up as physical pain in the muscles and joints. Sometimes it manifests as headaches, poor digestion, infections, or autoimmune diseases. Sometimes the trauma becomes part of how we interact with others and shows up as aggression, fear of being in strange places, claustrophobia, or post-traumatic stress disorder. With sexual trauma, there can also be specific sexual dysfunction and pain in the genital and anal areas that seem to have no medical cause. While addressing the physical aspects of these pains and discomforts is helpful, it is only part of the healing process.

For many people, talk therapy can be the perfect tool to

overcome and release those stuck places. Additional tools such as Eye Movement Desensitization and Reprogramming (EMDR) and Somatic Therapy can work in conjunction with talk therapy to quickly remove blocks to healing and allow the conscious mind to continue reweaving the new understanding into current behaviors and practices.

Eye Movement Desensitization and Reprocessing

EMDR is a therapeutic tool that enables people to heal from the physical and emotional symptoms that are the result of unresolved harmful experiences. Research shows that people from all walks of life and diverse trauma experiences can shift their symptoms in just a few sessions. It has been widely assumed that severe emotional pain is harder to heal than physical pain. EMDR therapy shows that the mind can heal from mental and emotional pain in similar ways to the healing of the body from an injury. When you cut your hand, your body works to close the wound. If a foreign object like dirt or microbes or repeated injury irritates the wound, it can become painfully infected. With cleaning and protection from reinjury, the body's healing response takes over.

EMDR therapy shows similarities occur with mental processes. The brain naturally moves toward mental health and balance by processing the distressing information and then letting it go. If the system is unable to work due to severity or recurrence of trauma, the emotional wound remains unhealed and can cause intense suffering. EMDR is used to remove the blocks to the brain's own processing systems and allows the trauma to be understood, integrated, and healed.

Somatic Therapy

Somatic Experiencing® was first introduced by Dr. Peter

Levine in the late 1970s and with the publication of his book, *Waking the Tiger: Healing Trauma*, in 1997 the popularity of his techniques expanded. From his observations of animal behavior in natural environments, he developed the theory that PTSD and similar health conditions are psychological manifestations of physical experiences. When we are threatened we go into fight, flight, or freeze mode, our survival brains take over, and we experience an enormous surge of energy as our system is flooded with the body chemicals needed to attack, escape, or play dead. If that energy isn't used in aggression or running away, it moves through the nervous system after the "freeze" mode is over through physical movements like shaking, yawning, tingling, or crying. If we are unable to fully discharge the energy, it leads to a disruption of our natural ability to heal. In nature, the healthy release of traumatic energy can be seen in animals who shake after escaping a predator. Our pets do the same thing. They shake or bark or yawn or urinate to release the tension after being in a confrontation—whether with another animal, the vacuum cleaner, or a large vehicle on the street.

The inability in people to complete the survival response can result from a number of causes. Children are particularly vulnerable, as they often have no option to fight or flee. In adults, both the nature of the trauma and the social stigma against "acting weird" by using physical expressions of energy release can keep us from our innate healing abilities. Somatic therapy is used by practitioners to safely lead the client mentally back to the feeling place of trauma in order to physically move the energy through the body and release it, which promotes healing.

Returning to Yourself

With patience and the care of a well-matched, caring, and

skilled counselor, learning new skills can empower us to do the sometimes difficult work of healing. Having a safe place to talk about pain and being willing to keep showing up for yourself can transform your ongoing story of pain so that you can find the place where those past experiences simply become a book on the shelf of your life library. Just because a book is on the shelf doesn't mean you have to read it. You know it is there. You can reference it as needed. You carry the wisdom of the learning with you so that you can free your mind, heart, and soul to keep writing the new books of the rest of your life and live in integrity of thoughts words and actions in alignment with your spiritual self.

We know we have healed a cut on our skin when the scab is gone and the new-grown skin has similar sensation to the surrounding, unharmed skin. Similarly, we know that painful experiences of our past have been healed when we can say no when we mean no and yes when we truly want what is offered. Healthy integration looks like making the choice to act differently when faced with a situation that reminds us of past pain and when we walk away from someone who doesn't value our full humanity.

Unpacking My Own Trunk of Pain

As I mentioned in the first chapter, I was raised in a conservative, religious home with parents who played out very traditional 1950s-style gender roles. My mother took care of all the emotional and day-to-day needs of the house, my father, and us kids and didn't do much for herself. My father earned the money, did the yard work, and maintained the mechanical systems of the house and cars. They worked together on our large garden, though not always at the same time. My siblings and I learned about much of the running of the household through observation and participation, much of it gendered between "men's work" and "women's work."

All that seemed to work for them as far as we knew. They rarely disagreed with each other in front of us. I did not witness my parents having an argument other than a difference in expected logistics of the house, i.e. my dad thought that things were going to happen in a certain order and my mom countered with a different plan. They sometimes had tight voices in those discussions, but I did not witness a disagreement that ended in anything other than "Oh, I guess we'll do it that way then." Any larger arguments were hidden, and I do not have any idea how they were then resolved. My parents did not talk about how to settle disagreements between ourselves or our friends other than "don't hit," "don't call names," "just ignore him/her." They yelled at us when they were angry, but never at each other. We were not allowed to yell at them, so we learned to suppress our anger or to let it out at our siblings.

I didn't even know how well I had absorbed this teaching until I was married and was afraid to disagree with my husband. I didn't even realize I was afraid of that until it showed up as physical pain and I had to deal with the issue. I found so much rage inside!

I discovered in therapy and by learning to observe my behavior that I was reacting to my husband's behavior in a similar way to the way I reacted to my father's behavior. Whereas my husband showed his anger and displeasure by becoming silent and shutting me out—the Cold War, as I called it—my father's style was a big yelling blowup followed by walking away or sending me to my room. He would then move on and within a few minutes he'd be acting like everything was normal. We didn't truly resolve anything because with my dad it was never a discussion. He didn't like my behavior; he yelled at me about it. I was expected to change my behavior to please him; we were done. Move on.

So, although my husband rarely yelled (which is what convinced me he wasn't like my dad at all), we danced around each other in much the same way. He would be angry with some aspect of my behavior; he would retreat behind a wall of silence. I would ask, cajole, beg for some indication of what made him angry; he would finally tell me... hours or days later. I was expected to apologize and change my behavior to please him; we moved on. I recall that I tried explaining my perspective to my husband just as I had with my father, but the result was the same. Neither one of those men changed their behavior. I was the one who made accommodations to keep the peace.

It took several years for me to unpack this steamer trunk of behaviors, reactions, provocations, and expectations—my codependence—both during my marriage and after we had separated. And, though I thought I had addressed my pain and learned how to do things differently, I found that my intimate relationships were giving me ample opportunities to continue to practice the new behaviors. I was faced with challenging situations that allowed me to ask for what I wanted, stop taking on all the responsibility for changing the dynamic that wasn't working, and break through the cycles of codependency that got in the way of true growth and change for both of us.

Here are some examples of what I mean:

I was partnered for five years with a woman whom I loved very much but who didn't allow herself to display her love in ways that felt empowering and validating to me. That's not to say she didn't love me. I believe that she did. However, she showed it sporadically and not often in front of other people. This was similar to my husband. Like him, she was very guarded and afraid of displaying too much emotion. However, because she was female, I let my expectation of how she could change belie the evidence of how she behaved. I also didn't want to tell the story of how I failed to keep another relationship alive.

I let my past experience of pain—feeling responsible and guilty about ending my marriage—run the relationship. I spent the last two years we were together doing everything I could imagine to reengage her, to make her fall in love with me again, to give her reasons not to leave even after she had emotionally checked out.

In another example, I dated a woman for a couple of months after crushing on her for eight years. She was a mess when we met: immature, alcoholic, and unreliable. I knew she wasn't good for me, but whenever I would see her—sometimes with years in between—I would feel my heart race, my stomach turn to butterflies, and my sexual energy rev up.

I ran into her at a comedy show one weekend and found that she had been sober for the previous two years. She suggested we go out, and within a few weeks we had created a cocoon of couplehood that didn't let in much logic or reason. Then, after another three weeks, she started acting peculiar and pulling away emotionally. When I confronted her about it, she downplayed my concerns, and I again let my past pain/training take control and shut my mouth instead of insisting that we talk things out until we both felt good about our relationship.

Within a week she had chosen to violate our agreement of monogamy and had sex with one of her coworkers, which she revealed to me two days later even though I could tell by her energy and behavior what she had done as soon as she came into my house the night it happened.

I wrestled with my pain all night long, and by the time she came over after work the following night, I was able to state my needs and wants clearly, calmly, and with integrity. Drama-free communication is an indicator of not letting pain run the show. I told her that I had not chosen to be in a polyamorous relationship with her coworker and that I was unwilling to continue our relationship. I felt very calm as she drove away, knowing I had taken a big step in affirming myself as a priority. The entire relationship lasted seven weeks.

Then I met a woman who had a history of trauma and mental illness, but when she was in a healthy emotional place, we got along very well. I fell in love with her potential—a recurring theme for me—and the person she showed me when she was feeling good about herself.

More often than not, though, her mental illness caused her to lash out, accusing me of all manner of behaviors that hurt her but which I had not actually done. As she demanded increasing reassurances and behavior changes, I realized that I could not ever be who she wanted me to be and still maintain my sense of self. I was able to connect the dots of my previous experience of pain, sidestep the reenactment of my painful behaviors, and walk away from the relationship.

Through those relationships and several others, I was able to practice staying aware of what my learned responses told me to do and to choose a different way of being. I had created new neural pathways and then repeated those behaviors so that I developed a new natural response. I allowed myself to question why some situations and conversations felt disempowering or frightening. Then I could choose to courageously face the pain that was being triggered so I could move through it and find another way of addressing the situation.

I learned to stop my knee-jerk reactions and stay present with the difficulty of someone else's pain without changing my behavior just so the other person would be comfortable for a few moments. Changing behavior eventually became something that was a true choice and sprouted from an agreement between both of us.

I had unlearned my learned codependence, and I continue to practice presence and listening so I continue growing. Often, my children were my biggest teachers and inspirations because I was determined to parent them differently than the way I had been guided. I can still recall how frightened I was to face my pain and seek a different path. I was sure I would lose everything I thought I had, but when I truly faced the situation, I realized that letting go of what I thought I had, opened up the space for me to reclaim my own space in my life and enter into relationships in which pain wasn't in charge of packing the bags.

QUESTIONS FOR REFLECTION

What patterns or repetitions do you recall from your own relationships?

How have you learned to avoid pain and discomfort?

Is there a small thing you could change to shift a pattern that doesn't make you feel good?

5
___

THE GARMENT BAG:

LET GO OF ASSUMPTIONS—ASK QUESTIONS INSTEAD

Assumptions allow the best in life to pass you by.
—John Sayles

ASSUMPTIONS ARE ONE OF THE LARGEST BAGS WE CARRY AROUND. This bag is packed with old experiences that we use to guess how new opportunities or situations could possibly affect us. Sometimes this can be helpful. If I vomited on a roller coaster before, I might assume that another roller coaster ride could garner the same result, so I'll be more careful in choosing a ride in the amusement park. In relationships, some assumptions can help us to sense danger, which can help us avoid unwanted pain.

As an example, in a discussion with a partner, coworker, friend, or parent, that person raises their voice or uses aggressive body language. You assume their behavior is a product of feeling angry or scared. You may sense that the other person might say or do something to hurt you or push you away, and so you modify your behavior to minimize the possibility of imminent danger.

However, like the beginning quote suggests, assumptions don't help build relationships. When I assume that my partner will act or react in a certain way, I close the doorway to the wide range of possible responses. Assumptions also stop us from asking questions.

Not all questions are helpful, though, in leading us to break out of patterns of thought or behavior that don't serve the situation or the people in it. Questions that don't work can be "What's wrong with you?" "Why are you acting just like your mother?" or "Why do you hate me?" These examples lead to defensiveness and lashing out. Questions like "Can you explain your feelings to me?" "How can I help you?" "Is my (or your) reaction coming from this situation or from a past hurt?" can all help to break up assumptions about the way things "should" be.

And while we are on the subject of *should*...

Think about how often the assumption of what someone "should" do, how you "should" feel, or what "should" happen in a given situation perpetuates a way of being that doesn't feel good. I try to use the word "should" as little as possible. "Should" slams the door of communication and opens the floodgate of guilt. As far as I know, no one has ever had a great relationship based on guilt.

Assumptions are like a curtain on a window. Sometimes that curtain is fairly thin, almost transparent. We can see through our assumptions of how the world is and figure out that the tall, thin object on the other side is a power pole and not a tree trunk, the light is the moon and not a streetlight, the four-legged animal is a deer on the lawn instead of a large dog. We can question our initial thoughts and revise our perceptions accordingly.

Those assumptions are fairly easy to dismantle. They may be assumptions like only white people can be leaders, women are naturally more emotional than men, or sex isn't interesting after age sixty. In each case, we can find ample evidence of the lie in the statement. People of all nationalities and ethnicities are wonderful leaders, men can and do have and express emotions as well as women (though many are encouraged or forced to deny their feelings). Additionally, if sex isn't interesting after sixty, then a whole lot of people are lying to me, and I don't think that's the case.

Other assumptions are more difficult to see and dismantle. These are the curtains that block out light, that don't allow us to see another perspective unless there is an open window and a stiff wind or because we actively choose to pull back the curtain and examine both the assumption-curtain and the view we find behind it.

The more difficult assumptions are the ones that remind us of our own trauma held over from painful past events. If you have been hurt in a previous relationship through infidelity, you may be vigilant about being harmed similarly in a new relationship. This vigilance may lead you to assume that your new lover's way of being friendly and welcoming to many people is a signal that he intends to leave you or is seeking other lovers because he is not very interested in you. You may be accusatory and suspicious when you see your lover greeting friends or new acquaintances with warmth and affection because you don't trust his words of assurance that you are the person he wants. You stop asking questions of him because you think he is lying, and you stop asking questions of yourself to learn why you don't trust him. This is when you get to make a choice whether to start asking the helpful questions or not.

It can be scary to ask questions because the answers could be uncomfortable. Answers give us information, and that information may not be what we want to hear. We may have to keep asking questions that bring about change, and change can be just as scary as the information we discover. However, true intimacy comes from revealing who we are and what we want to another person. We take the risk that the other person may decide that the information we have revealed isn't what they want to hear or isn't something that they are willing to accept. It can seem easier to just cut things off the first time they become uncomfortable.

As children we build our worldview from things we are told by adults, behaviors we observe in the people around us, and our own experiences. If we live in an area where most of the families seem to be very similar to our own, we learn to assume that other people think and react much the same way as we do. When we grow up, we can be amazed to learn that other people have different views and experiences, especially when those other people look similarly and come from superficially similar backgrounds to ourselves. It's easy to imagine that someone from another country or another culture could have different experiences and form a different worldview. What is often more difficult to grasp is that each family has its own culture, history, and expectations of behavior. From those familial differences we are all living with assumptions we might not have ever questioned but that are keeping us from truly understanding a partner.

So how do you start asking questions to unpack the baggage of assumptions? One of the places to start can be to look at your family of origin and the patterns of behavior around activities or actions. Here are a few to start you off.

- How did your family handle large gatherings or celebrate holidays and other big events? Do you do things exactly the same way? Why or why not?
- How did you learn to handle conflict as a child? Do you still handle conflict this way?
- What were your family's rules for behavior in public, at home, or with guests? Have you changed the rules for yourself?

- What did you learn about relationships from observing your parents, relatives, and other adults?
- What messages about sexuality did you receive?
- What did spirituality mean, and how was it expressed by those around you?
- How might you be using those assumptions in your relationships? Can you ask questions to get more insight into another person's behavior and motivation?

This is also the time when talking with a professional counselor can be very helpful. Sometimes asking these questions can feel very scary. You may have some fears in thinking about your childhood. You may have difficulty managing your emotions if you learn that you are behaving in ways you don't like. You may also find that your assumptions led to incorrect views of others' behaviors. It can feel unsettling or scary to realize you were wrong or that you taught yourself to ignore certain behaviors and messages. Don't let your fears stop you from growing. Find someone who can help you unpack these bags of assumptions and start asking questions of yourself. When you find clarity in your own assumptions and motivations, it will be easier to ask questions of others.

Narrowing the frame of assumptions to focus on the physical body and sexuality, we find that repression is often present. The brain, which holds on to assumptions, is our biggest sex organ, and the complex network of memories, thoughts, neural responses, and interactions in the brain can contribute to the baggage we carry. When we repress our questions and operate on assumptions, it can feel like shoving our feelings and hurts and shame into a small space inside, hiding them away so we don't have to deal with them.

Eventually most of us will be clued into the burgeoning baggage because our bodies will show us that something is wrong through painful sex, dysfunction or disinterest in physical pleasure, or pushing us into risky situations so we can feel alive again.

Assumptions can also lead to painful re-creations of past situations. When we assume that a new lover will be different than previous lovers, we often avoid asking questions about their experiences and expectations. We jump headlong into the hormone-filled ocean of lust and sometimes ignore the red flags that are present, warning us of danger. The danger flags can be instances of controlling behavior or times when you feel ignored or diminished by your new partner when out in public. The danger flags could look like not checking in with you about your desires for affection, sexual expression, or your enjoyment of sexual activities. The assumption that the new face means new and different behaviors belies the all-too-familiar reality that you've chosen a partner similar to past partners because you recognize on an unconscious level that those are behaviors and responses that you are called to heal within yourself.

Consent

One of the central factors in diffusing assumptions is the notion of consent. Given the expansion of the #MeToo movement as a way of raising awareness about sexual harassment and abuse in the workplace, consent has been given a much larger spotlight in the past few years than ever before. Children as young as three years old are being taught to ask before giving their friends hugs and not just assuming that hugging or touching is okay. Adults are being told that children do not owe them hugs or kisses because they are relatives or longtime family friends. Consent has become a central part of many sex education curricula, as well as being included in workplace trainings across industries.

As a way to understand the importance of consent, there was a wonderful example created in 2015 as a cartoon about making someone a cup of tea by Emmaline May of RockStarDinosaur-PiratePrincess and Blue Seat Studios. I encourage you to find this and watch it, if you've not done so already. In the cartoon, initiating sex is compared to offering someone a cup of tea. If you get an enthusiastic yes, then go ahead and make the tea. If the person isn't superexcited about tea but doesn't give an outright "no," then you can make the tea, but you cannot force the person to drink it. If the response is "I don't want any tea," then you stop offering. Finally, if the person initially says, "Sure, tea would be great," or something that conveys agreement but then decides that they don't want tea after you've made it, you do not force them to drink the tea. People are allowed to change their minds about tea... and about sex... and about everything else, really.

So, consent is the awareness and willingness to accept an offer. Since we're talking about sex here, consent to be sexual can only be truly given by a conscious, mentally capable, adult human being. Drunk or high people, children, people with severe mental health issues, traumatic brain injury or significant learning disabilities, ill people, people who are in danger, people who are asleep or unconscious, and people who are being cajoled by a person of greater power *cannot* give full consent for sexual activity on any level. They cannot give enthusiastic agreement with full awareness of what is being asked. Additionally, consent can be rescinded at any point for any reason by any individual.

The caring and ethical lover respects consent and the ability to set and accept boundaries. There are no assumptions that are more important than asking the questions that lead to understanding your partner as a full and willing participant. If you have been operating under certain assumptions, as many of us do, it is time to develop a practice of asking questions both of yourself and of your partner(s) that will lead you to deeper wisdom about your behaviors, your desires, and your roles in relationships. This is the time to tune into your heart and let go of the ego's desire for importance and power. Your heart knows the truth that shared power builds intimacy and allows both people to stand in their integrity being honored as the divine humans we are.

Randall and Bonnie's Story

Randall and Bonnie had been very happily married for sixteen years when they hit a bump or—as Bonnie put it—a warning bell. A mutual friend of theirs, Katie, whom they had known for several years, started to express romantic interest in Bonnie. Both Bonnie and Katie identified as bisexual and had dated both women and men before marrying their husbands. Katie had divorced her husband a couple of years before she approached Bonnie. Randall had only ever dated women, but he was interested in exploring nontraditional relationships. In their initial conversations, Katie admitted that she was also attracted to Randall. Both Bonnie and Randall thought it would be fun to include Katie in their sexual explorations, and the three began to discuss the parameters of open relationship.

About six months after this new paradigm commenced, things started to feel tense between Randall and Bonnie. They tried to shift things around and recapture the initial excitement, but they weren't finding it, and the stress was showing. That's when they came to me.

We began by talking about what drew them into agreeing to accept Katie into their previously closed relationship. Like many couples who choose to explore opening their relationship to other lovers, Randall and Bonnie were looking for a way to enhance their sex life in a way that would allow them to see each other in a new light. Unlike many couples who start experimenting with polyamory, Bonnie and Randall were very satisfied with the sex they shared and were not looking for another person to distract them from each other and gloss over problems that were present. In many ways they were the ideal couple to open up into a polyamorous relationship because their dyad was strong, they had excellent communication, and they had a very robust and enjoyable sex life.

The bump came about because Katie was asking for more one-on-one time with each of them, and they had been dealing with feelings of jealousy and anger toward each other and toward Katie that they had not been addressing. Randall assumed that Bonnie was enjoying her time with Katie more than was true for Bonnie. He thought that their marriage was being put on the back burner, and though that was bothersome to him, he didn't question Bonnie because he wanted her to continue enjoying her relationship with Katie. Bonnie was assuming much the same thing. She also was feeling manipulated by Katie, but she didn't want to worry Randall who, she thought, was very happy with the arrangement and all the sex they were having.

For the greater portion of their marriage, one of their strengths was their ability to communicate, but in the process of the new excitement with Katie, they stopped checking in with each other and started to think of themselves as a trio rather than a couple plus one. Both types of relationships are workable, but trios require a different type of communication than couple plus one. In an ideal trio, each person is the equal partner of both other people, which isn't always easy to maintain, but we're talking best-case scenario here. In a couple plus one, the couple agrees to allow the third person partial access into their dyad but not full partnership.

Bonnie and Randall had initially agreed to the couple-plus-one dynamic, and Katie had agreed to their request. As time went on, everyone seemed to be enjoying themselves, and Katie started spending more and more time at their home in nonsexual ways—just hanging out. Bonnie and Randall told me that initially that closeness had felt sweet and comfortable, but in recent weeks, Bonnie had begun to feel that Katie was trying to isolate Randall and draw his attention in ways that excluded Bonnie. She also thought that Katie was not sharing time with Bonnie in the way she had at the beginning. Bonnie and Randall had stopped having regular check-ins about the state of their marriage, and Bonnie was missing her husband's touch and attention.

During our sessions, I led them in exercises that allowed them to talk about what assumptions they were carrying concerning long-term couplehood, what being jealous felt like, and what behaviors were coming out as a result of being jealous rather than simply asking for what they each wanted. We worked on the assumptions of dating, since they hadn't had to deal with those for over a decade, and how that new-relationship energy can lead to glossing over places of discomfort that would be better served by asking questions for clarification. Randall admitted that he enjoyed seeing Bonnie and Katie being sexual together. He often didn't say anything when he wanted to participate because he assumed that Bonnie was preferring sex with Katie since she hadn't been sexual with a woman during their sixteen years of marriage.

Bonnie had been reluctant to tell Randall of her waning interest in Katie because she didn't want to face the possibility that Randall was still very interested in their arrangement. She assumed that, given a choice, Randall might choose to continue seeing Katie because she was the "new girl." Both of them were using assumptions to predict what the other was feeling or wanting. They were both fearful of asking questions because they might not like the answers, but the fear was keeping them both in a place that fostered more fear. Katie was only partially aware of what was going on with them and was also living with her own desires and feelings.

We worked together for only six sessions spaced out every other week over three months. Bonnie and Randall mostly needed reminders of how to communicate and some new questions to ask before they were back on track with each other and finding their footing again. They each recommitted to their primary relationship with each other. They decided individually and not at the same time to break things off with Katie.

Bonnie told Katie that she was feeling too drained by Katie's need for ongoing deep, emotional connection and sexy playtime and that Bonnie wanted to focus her emotional energy on Randall. A couple of months later, Randall decided that being monogamous with Bonnie was better for their marriage, though Bonnie had not issued any ultimatums about Randall seeing Katie. During the time when only Randall was seeing Katie, Bonnie saw me individually to work on staying in her truth about what she wanted from her marriage and how she wanted to show up. We practiced setting boundaries, especially saying "No, I don't want to do that" without going into long explanations that can weaken boundaries while also staying open to conversations that were uncomfortable.

What Bonnie and Randall found was that their unspoken ideas about what marriage meant, what monogamy meant, and what sex meant both within and outside their marriage were so deeply buried that they didn't even think to ask some of the questions that I had brought up in our sessions. And they each assumed that the other person had the same ways of thinking. Given that they each had different families and came from different cultures within the United States, I wasn't surprised that they had different perspectives

One of the things that Bonnie assumed was that because they had been married for sixteen years, Randall would—should —know that Bonnie wanted extra reassurance from him as they experimented with new activities that included sex with Katie. Bonnie's family was very verbal about checking in with each other in many ways and would do new things slowly with lots of verbal processing. Randall knew this, but in the excitement and novelty of opening up their dyad, he also assumed that Bonnie would be just as excited as he was. Randall's family was adventurous and was always planning new trips and exotic vacations. He grew up with less verbal processing because his parents just kept encouraging the kids to "jump right in" and "try new things." Neither of these approaches is wrong, but they are different. Each person's approach was so much a part of their individual worldview that neither one thought to ask the questions that might have helped them navigate the relationship shift with a little more clarity and support from each other.

Today Randall and Bonnie are still happily married and about to celebrate their twenty-seventh wedding anniversary. They learned a lot about each other and about themselves during and after their time with Katie. They learned that they each carry more assumptions about how they viewed relationships and sexuality than they had imagined. They learned that it is okay to ask questions so that they could learn more about each other and that asking questions does not equal accusations of doing something wrong. They also found ways to communicate that gave them each more space for questioning their own assumptions and creating deeper intimacy by revealing the parts of themselves that had been hidden from the other person.

QUESTIONS FOR REFLECTION

Think about how your parents, grandparents, and other relatives or close adults behaved in their relationships. What are some similarities and differences between how they related and how you relate to your significant other or others?

Did you have any strong reactions when reading about Randall and Bonnie? What were they? Why do you think you may feel that way?

Can you think of times when you have asked a question or questions that allowed you to let go of assumptions about others or about yourself?

6

THE BOARDING BAG:

PRESENCE INSTEAD OF PERFORMANCE

It is not sex that gives the pleasure, but the lover.
—Marge Piercy

MOVIES, BOOKS, SONGS, AND OTHER CULTURAL EXPRESSIONS HAVE perpetuated the myth that there is one "right" way to make love. This right way often involves the meeting of the eyes, the kissing, the undressing, the lovemaking in one to three positions culminating in simultaneous orgasm followed by the snuggling and falling asleep together. This is primarily a heterosexual design in which the man pursues the woman, though she demurs. He is persistent, insistent, and charming so she agrees to sex, which affirms how much she wanted him all along. All this is accompanied by appropriately romantic background music to disguise the reality of bodily noises, pets and/or children in the same location, or having to communicate with a new partner. Unless you're watching a romantic comedy and "bad" sex is used as a plot device to elongate the story, sex seems to be easy and perfect from the beginning.

We've grown up with multiple versions of this pattern. The fairy tales tell us nothing about sex but suggest that once any initial obstacles are gone, "They lived happily ever after." Many songs and films are equally vague, though some are explicit in just exactly what sex play the narrator, character, or singer wants and expects to get. Very few actually describe what goes into healthy sex and healthy relationships.

Presence—fully inhabiting your body and soul and listening to your partner—will contribute more to your sexual relationship and spiritual connection than any athletic-inspired, porn-informed, movie-ready performance you can dream up.

Real life and relationships with real people can be intimidating and make us feel like something is wrong—with ourselves, our partners, or the situation. Be honest. How often has this ideal scenario actually occurred for you? Do you walk around with romantic music at the ready just in case you see a beautiful stranger at the bank, the copy machine at work, or the grocery store? Does every delivery person or maintenance person coming to your door look at you with "come hither" eyes and sexual energy? Probably not.

We are learning that our cultural programming that tells men that "no" from a woman really means "keep trying and I'll change my mind" actually inhibits the ability to create a relationship of equality and intimacy. Not listening and pushing your own agenda conveys lack of respect and contributes to feelings of distrust and fear in your desired partner.

Good sex and real intimacy come when you show up fully as your perfectly imperfect self and encourage your partner to do the same. Unpacking the performance bag allows a vast range of sexual experiences to fall into the "right" way to do things. Every body is different, and while many of us have similar erotic ideas, sensations, and preferred activities, the way in which we each respond to sexual stimuli—aka the arousal response—is not exactly like anyone else.

For example, the story of women's responsiveness to nipple stimulation is not every woman's experience. Some women are not turned on at all by nipple play, and others find even the slightest touch borders on discomfort due to extrasensitive nipples. Additionally, men are rarely depicted as having enjoyable nipple sensations, but many men can and do enjoy nipple play and find it highly erotic. If you are focused on re-creating the perfect story or situation, you will miss the cues of your lover's body and sacrifice pleasure and connection, trying to give the performance you imagine is required. Sexual pleasure does not rely on an A-plus performance but on the soulful presence of the people involved, whether that involvement is for an hour, a season, or many years.

When you are focused on enjoying yourself and enjoying the person or people you are with, then sex is not about an Academy Award performance, viral clip on YouTube, or the reenactment of a scene from your favorite sexy book. Sexual expression—living fully as your spiritual sexual self—is not a performance limited to a certain time and place. It is who you are: a range of behaviors and responses expressed in different ways at different times with different people. Your sexual expression is completely unique to you. The range is wide because there is no right way to experience sexual pleasure.

Some ways to examine the range of sexual activities that you do like or might like and which ones are fun and exciting for your partner can be found in the appendix. My Sexual Activities Checklist, which I referenced earlier, gives you a great place to start unpacking your sexual performance baggage by asking you to determine whether the activity described is something you have done or not, liked or not, or were unsure about and perhaps willing to try. If you do the list on your own, you will have a visual representation of part of your sexual road map, and you can use that to talk with your partner or potential partner about your likes and desires. It's a great tool for couples as well. Once you have completed the checklist individually, compare your answers to learn more about what you like and want, what you may be interested in exploring together, and some possible areas of sensitivity that may be triggering your arguments or avoidance.

Keep in mind the Sexual Activities Checklist is not a rating system! Sex from a place of presence cannot be rated on any sort of scale except personal pleasure, which is completely internal. When you are focusing on your sexual performance, however, there is the danger of feeling rated because one aspect of performance is the rating. A performance has to be externally rated, often by others—or the voices of others in our heads—to have value, doesn't it? There has to be delineation between great, good, average, and poor. How else would we know who wins? Unfortunately, we often rate ourselves as average or poor and then treat ourselves as the losers we think we are.

In the previous chapter, I talked about letting go of assumptions and asking questions. The same techniques can be used here to open the performance bag to allow us to gauge whether we are trying to play by someone else's rules or cultivating presence and being true to ourselves. Questioning courageously—seeking true answers—is the key to opening and unpacking each piece of our sexual baggage and all other baggage as well.

Oftentimes the question to start with is: Why am I feeling unsatisfied? Rather than resort to the easy answer and blame it all on your partner, you can use this question to examine what "being satisfied" means to you. Does satisfaction come from another person, or does it come from within? Does your pleasure and satisfaction feel greatest when it comes from a place where you and your partner are working and loving together in a deeply connected way, or does it come from an idea of being the World's Greatest Lover?

You can take this exploration deeper by seeking to know the thoughts you think when being sexual. Do you think of how your lover is admiring you, your looks, your skills? Do you think of what new tricks or techniques you can do to surprise and please your lover? Do you strike poses that you know make you look your best more often than you simply allow your body to be present with its imperfections?

Letting go of performance-based thinking means allowing all those judgmental thoughts to come in and then go right out. You can help this along by checking in with your partner to learn more about their experience. Is your partner enjoying herself? Are you able to find excitement in small movements as well as larger ones? Do you feel connected, or are you trying to re-create some position or scenario that you saw in a movie or on some online video and have lost touch with your connection with each other?

Pornography is rarely about presence. If you got much of your sex education via porn, you might be missing out on a huge part of the pleasure of being sexual. Pornography is designed to produce the fastest response in the least amount of time. It bombards the viewer with scene after scene of decadent, acrobatic, penis-centered exploits, but rarely does anyone seem to be enjoying the process or the person with whom they are sharing the scene. In mainstream movies, the buildup of sexual tension via an obstacle (i.e. they are on opposite sides of an argument, their families don't want them together, there is an established relationship that should not be violated—married, boss/employee, teacher/student, etc.) is the point, and once that tension is broken via sexual contact, there is usually a short wrap-up to see the couple together before the movie ends, or there is another problem that keeps them apart for a while longer. That story arc does not advocate for presence either.

On the surface, presence can seem too simple. It's just about being with someone, right? Yes, *and* it is also much more than that. Presence means you show up and bring all of yourself. You allow for differences in desire on a given day and you find a place of connection within that disparity. You accept that sometimes you're angry with each other, and you do the work to understand where the anger starts and how to resolve it. You realize that each person has body parts they don't love, and you accept them and yourself just as you are. More on this in the next chapter.

Presence means having healthy boundaries so that you don't exhaust yourself by overgiving until you are trying to get water from an empty well. It means you don't pretend to be excited when you are not but that you also don't wait for everything to be perfect before you can be in the mood. Presence means being honest about your situation, your feelings, your health status, your willingness to participate, your intention for long-term relationship, and your desires. It means listening to your lover and honoring their words and their body language. Presence asks for all of yourself: not just the pretty parts, the athletic parts, the great-skills-in-bed parts, or the I-just-want-to-please-you parts.

Cultivating Presence

To be present with yourself is one part of learning to be present with another person. They are complimentary practices, but we are told that we have to "be there" for others far more than we are reminded to "be there" for ourselves. In order to truly be with someone else, however, you must learn to be present with and for yourself. As in the previous chapters, we are adding to your tools and skills to help you hone your effectiveness in being present.

In Chapter Two, I shared my breathing practice for becoming more embodied. Practicing presence is much the same, but this practice has the additional layer of awareness of where you are in the world along with the embodiment awareness of feeling into your skin. Though it may seem obvious to say, being present means being exactly where you are in your body, your mind, and your spirit as well as in the world around you, whether that is a bedroom, a courtroom, a confessional, an amusement park, or a hospital waiting room. Being present means that you're not trying to re-create or reinvent the past, nor are you worrying and planning for the future. You are simply here. Right here, right now, aware of yourself and the person or people around you.

Five-minute Presence Practice

1. Become aware of where you are. Feel your feet on the ground as you stand or the pressure on your back, buttocks, and legs from the seat on which you're sitting. Breathe and notice any sensations that are present.

2. Listen to the sounds around you as you continue to breathe. Note what they are, but don't think too hard about it.

3. Look at the details of your surroundings. Just notice what is there without trying to name it all or get caught up in a thought thread.

4. Note any odors or tastes you detect.

5. Feel your clothing touching your skin. Note any airflow or other sensations on your skin.

6. As you breathe, let any thoughts that arise be noted and then let them go. This is not the time to delve into a daydream or plan your next activity. You are practicing being fully aware of the present moment, and thoughts are most often about the past or the future.

7. From this place of presence you'll probably feel calm and centered. If that is not the case, now is the time to ask internal questions about your thoughts and feelings to discover what is pulling you away from the present.

8. When you have fully immersed your awareness in the here and now, you have become present. This is the feeling place

from which I encourage you to begin when you are with a partner.

Presence Practice for Two

1. Use the above steps with your partner when you are beginning a sexual activity. Work with each other to become fully present in the moment. Tune into each other's breathing, sounds, and body language.

2. As you continue with your physical actions and feel the arousal build, bring yourself back to being present whenever you notice that you are wondering how you look, if you're doing enough, or trying to guess what your partner is thinking or feeling.

3. When you have questions about what your partner is experiencing, ask them. It's okay to talk during sex even if it seems like you might kill the mood. Far better to ask the question and get an answer than to get caught up in overthinking.

Cultivating presence is spiritual, lifelong work, but it becomes easier and easier the more you practice. Eventually you'll find that not being present is actually difficult and uncomfortable. You'll avoid those people who don't encourage you to be fully present because you'll realize that they are not fully present themselves. Your sexual experiences will become richer and more meaningful, even if they aren't going to win any Sexiest Person Alive or Most Valuable Player awards. You'll realize that being truly with someone—whether long-term partner or new acquaintance—is what makes the sexual experience wonderful regardless of how many orgasms are had or if you re-created a fantasy perfectly. You'll know that because you showed up with your full self... body, mind, and soul; you had sex the "right" way.

GEOFF'S STORY

Geoff was used to being viewed as a very handsome man. When he walked into my office, he was confident and poised. In fact, his posture seemed practiced and displayed, as if he expected someone was holding a camera to take his photograph. He was so used to getting attention for his looks that he wasn't present in his body. His mind was focused on my reaction to him, which I understood when he told me how much his jacket had cost and how his boyfriend had picked it out for him. I didn't know if he was trying to impress me with the label, if he was trying to impress me with his boyfriend's devotion, or if he was hoping that we would talk about his looks or style instead of why he was coming to see me. After a few minutes of conversation, I asked him what part of his heart hurt enough to want to see me.

Geoff was quiet for several minutes. His face seemed to shift and droop, and his shoulders sagged a bit. He took a breath and then said he wasn't sure he could keep up with his boyfriend's expectations around sex. I asked him to explain, and he talked about how his boyfriend, Eric, was always turned on, wanted sex multiple times each week, and was very excited about role-playing. Geoff wasn't always in the mood when Eric was. He had a busy job and was often called on to care for his aging parents because his sister traveled frequently. Also, Geoff was fifty-three and Eric was thirty-six.

Geoff felt that even though they had been together for five years, Eric still lived in the fantasy of first romance and expected dating-type sex, whereas Geoff was ready to relax a bit and not have to keep up with the courtship model of sexual adventure. He complained of being tired of having to come up with scenarios and costumes, of having to "plan" to be spontaneous, of feeling like the onus of seduction was always on him.

Over the next few months, we discussed ways in which Geoff could open up to Eric about his feelings of having to perform, of always being ready, and of the deeper intimacy he was craving. Having to be sexual in a way that re-created their early dating days was leaving Geoff feeling drained and not sexy, but he was afraid of telling Eric. He was afraid that Eric wouldn't want an old man who couldn't have sex as often as Eric wanted. Geoff had to open up to what his true desires were and face his inner critic, who was telling him that sex was great if it lasted a certain length of time, involved fantasy exploration, or if there were certain goals attained. His inner voice of criticism deemed sex only fair or poor if those criteria were not met.

I suggested homework practices to help Geoff get in touch with his body again. Some included walking barefoot on the grass in their yard, deep belly breathing to help him slow down his thoughts, yoga and stretching routines, and sitting with his eyes closed outside or inside and focusing on what he could hear, see, and touch. I also recommended that Geoff and Eric stop having sex for a month to relearn sensual, nonsexual touch through Sensate Focus exercises that I provided. The exercises helped them to remember how they used to pay attention to body cues like breathing, muscle relaxation, soft sighs, as well as words to guide where each one wanted to be touched. They were encouraged to explore those sensual touches more deeply and then connect that knowledge to sex as they resumed that part of touching.

Geoff and Eric started talking about desire in a new way. They expressed what each of them truly wanted from their sex life and how to keep their expectations in check. We worked on practicing presence with each part of their sexual encounters so that Geoff could stay in his body and out of the judgmental part of his brain that kept up the evaluation of performance.

By slowing down their sex and being more sensual, Geoff

and Eric found a new level of intimacy, and Geoff found new energy for sex play. He was able to say yes to sex in a new way because, as he reported, not every time had to be an "Olympic performance with a judge and score card." When Geoff found that his ability to talk about sex changed, his ability to "do" sex became more about who he was and who he wanted to be as part of a couple and not only about what he did with, for, and to Eric in bed.

QUESTIONS FOR REFLECTION

When did you realize that movie depictions of sex were unreal? How did that affect your interactions?

How do you evaluate sex to decide if it is good?

Looking back at your most recent sexual activity, were you *performing* or *experiencing*? How do you know? Could you do something differently next time to be more present?

7

THE DUFFEL BAG:

GREAT SEX, SELF-ESTEEM, AND BODY IMAGE

You yourself, as much as anybody in the entire universe, deserve your love and affection.
—Buddha

IN A PERFECT WORLD, WE WOULD SPEND OUR EARLIEST YEARS knowing without question that we are valuable and lovable. We would have parents and other family members who show us and tell us that we are smart, beautiful, strong, capable, and helpful.

As babies, we came into this world assuming that we were worthy of all good things: all the love, all the joy, and all the pleasure we could fit into our little bodies. Before we knew words, we knew our worth. We reached out for touch, we hugged and kissed with abandon, we snuggled our animal friends. Many of us took for granted that others would reach out to us and say loving words.

That is the way it's supposed to be for our whole lives: accepted, celebrated, and loved. Yet as we grow and encounter people who don't love us, we start to question our self-worth. It happens almost as soon as we find ourselves in a group setting such as a preschool or kindergarten class, perhaps sooner.

- Does Mommy love the new baby more than me?
- Why does Daddy play games with my brother more?
- Is she smarter than me?
- Is he faster than me?
- Does the teacher pay more attention to her?

Our feelings of self-worth become dependent on whether or not we get an extra scoop of ice cream, a sterner reprimand, a higher or lower grade on a test, a new pair of shoes, hand-me-down jeans, or a place on the team of our choice. We learn shame when we are told that we are bad for behaving or speaking in ways that go against adults' rules. Parents, caregivers, and teachers may try to be fair, to treat all their children the same, but that never works because all children are different and adults are people who come with their own expectations, limitations, and baggage.

Life is truly fair when everyone is getting what they need, not when everyone is treated exactly the same. This definition is not often explained to children or even to adults. This fallacy of blanket equality belies our true need to be seen and valued for our individual selves. From a small but noticeable stream in childhood and increasing to full blast when we enter puberty, we simultaneously want to be just like our peers and also be noticed as someone special and unique. The intense emotions brought about by the hormonal bath during puberty make everything feel like a confusing competition where the rules change often and are rarely fair. Sometimes the winner is the one who is pretty, sometimes the smartest kid is the best, sometimes none of that matters if you don't have the most stylish clothes or shoes or the newest electronics.

The hierarchy of adolescence and adulthood is a system wherein those who are on top are terrified of losing their status while those on the lower tiers are envious of those above and disdainful of those perceived to be below them. Fear runs the show, and most people spend years doing whatever they can to maintain their place or rise in status because their inner monologue tells them that they aren't good enough. If you're not worthy of getting notice or approval for these outside achievements like clothing, gadgets, beauty, or physical prowess, it is difficult to feel worthy of love and acceptance when it comes to the vulnerability inherent in exploring sexuality.

Let's assume you've made it through elementary school relatively unscathed in your self-esteem. Here you are, eleven or twelve years old (or older or younger depending on your unique experience) in the throes of your first major attraction. Some might call it puppy love, but you know it's the real deal. Of course it is! Love is not more or less real because you are a certain age.

Your body is on fire with desire for touch, for kissing, for you're-not-sure what because you've never felt this way before, and any kind of interaction with someone attractive sends your hormones rocketing to the moon. Your body is demanding to be pleasured and to give pleasure, and you search around for someone who can explore those feelings with you. When you set your sights on someone and project all your longings onto them, you create a story that tells you that if the person you love doesn't love you back, you'll want to just die.

You get wrapped up in what your friends say you need, what cultural references like movies, television shows, and music tell you about love and sex, and you're absolutely sure that you can't ask an adult about this because all these feelings are so new and intense you don't even know how to verbalize them—and adults never understand anyway. You might have been told you shouldn't think about it because it is bad or sinful or that you're too young to feel this way. You spend hours imagining scenarios of physical closeness and tender words.

At some point you may decide to speak up and tell that attractive person how you feel. Ideally, she or he responds with words that validate your worth and your feelings. Many times, however, the outcome is different.

Childhood is rarely that idyllic. For most of us, we are part of a culture that looks for ways to keep us from getting "too big for our britches." We receive blow after blow to our self-esteem through bullying or self-comparison. We have a weird family, are too poor, too stupid, too religious, not religious enough, gay or lesbian, homeless. Our bodies are denigrated as too fat, too skinny, not enough curves or not the "right" ones, not strong enough, not athletic enough, too dark, too pale, zits, bad hair, too loud, too weird, disabled. These words can wound, and if repeated, as they often are, can leave scars in our psyches that inhibit our ability to believe that we are inherently worthy of great love—physically, emotionally, and spiritually.

What happens when you believe the lies others have told you about yourself from the perspective of their own distortions and pain?

Once you confront the fact that you were lied to, how do you rebuild your self-esteem and claim your worthiness for love and sexual connection?

You start by acknowledging the falseness of these beliefs. There are always going to be people who are different from you. Difference does not make some someone inherently better or worse as a person. Those judgments are lies of oppression. Some people are physically stronger or faster than others. Some folks are better at thinking on their feet or enjoy speaking in public. There are people who have a talent for creating new computer software, being excellent teachers, or have the ability to drive long distances and maneuver large equipment. Some people cannot walk with ease or speak distinctly; others are learning a new language. Few people fully conform to beauty trends or media ideals, and bodies come in lots of shapes and sizes. None of these differences prevents someone from being lovable or attractive.

What does get in the way of seeing ourselves as lovable or attractive is our beliefs both about our worth and about our ability to give and receive love from others. With so many messages swirling around about what is attractive, who or what is desirable, and the added factor of shame for whatever we might have experienced, it can feel overwhelming to even begin to unpack this bag. Sometimes the unpacking and examining of our beliefs needs to happen in a subtle way rather than flat-out contradiction of the lies. We can start with asking questions such as:

If I did believe I was worthy of love, how might I act?

I wouldn't talk to a friend this way, so why do I say these things about myself?

Being able to take a step back from the story of our unworthiness creates a space to find the parts of ourselves that we do like, value, and can share with others. Then when self-sabotage comes in, we have a place to return to for observation rather than descend into the pit of despair and recriminations that reinforce the lie. We don't have to use the tactics of the hierarchy by only choosing relationships with someone who "needs" us, thereby fostering unhealthy codependence. Reclaiming self-worth is a process of opening up the bags labeled NOT GOOD ENOUGH, and WHY CAN'T I BE DIFFERENT to release the lies that we've tucked away through believing that someone else gets to dictate our fitness for relationship and love.

What an empowering feeling it is to meet someone new and know that you are worthy of your own love and appreciation and not dependent on whether or not that person desires you to prove anything! This isn't about replacing the lies of "too ugly, too skinny, too weird, too... whatever" with upholding an illusion of perfection either. Self-esteem comes from understanding that you are perfectly imperfect just as you are. Your body will always have parts that some people find fabulous and others find less appealing. You are not attracted to everyone you meet. Every person on the street is not your "flavor," nor are you the favorite "flavor" for all others. Thank goodness! How exhausting would it be to feel attracted to everyone in your path or to have all people you see each day fall over themselves with desire for you?

Self-esteem is about regarding yourself with love, kindness, and honor for all the beautiful, awkward, messy, and brilliant spiritual human-ness you carry with you. It's about being gentle with yourself when you don't live up to your highest ideals, and it's about holding firm to your boundaries so you don't give away more than you want. Self-esteem is admiring your strengths, honoring your limitations, and understanding that you have the power to receive love and desire just as much as you can give those things too. It is the deep-bone knowing that you are a soul with a body, a body with a soul, a spark of divine love and grace living an embodied human life worthy of celebration and awe.

When you find that place of truly liking who you are, you may occasionally notice holdover thoughts that try to derail you from feeling good about yourself. Having unpacked these bags, though, will allow you to put those thoughts in the light of your observation and ask: Is this true? Do I actually believe this, or is this idea a lie that someone else told me was true? It's much easier to discard those old thoughts once you recognize them for the falsehoods they are.

The Bodies We Have

Aging bodies. One of the falsehoods we learn is that being old is a turnoff. Wrinkles, gray hair, teeth that are not blindingly white, limited vision, joint pain and muscle weakness, or any other sign that you are old is depicted as a reason to be depressed, jealous of others, and to seek out expensive and sometimes dangerous treatments and procedures that claim to halt or reverse the signs of aging. There comes a point in each of our lives when we become aware that we are not getting attention in the same way. It can be a blow to our self-esteem, especially if we have been accustomed to being seen as attractive and sexually desirable for much of our lives.

The truth is that many people remain sexually active or even increase their desire in their senior years, but that may go unnoticed by a culture that puts most of the focus on young faces and bodies. Self-esteem is strengthened by remembering who we are, what we have learned, and how to dress and adorn our bodies in ways that celebrate our maturity and wisdom, not by trying to compete with people who are decades younger.

Sexual activity looks different over fifty as well. We may not be able to move in the ways we could in previous years. We may have health issues that compromise stamina, breathing, or positioning. Men may experience differences in erection strength and duration, and women may experience vaginal dryness or vulvar pain after menopause. Part of accepting our bodies is acknowledging what is different and being honest with partners about modifications and challenges.

Fat bodies. Fat is one of the leading reasons women and men report for feeling uncomfortable in their bodies. According to statistics compiled by the National Association of Anorexia Nervosa and Associated Disorders, 70 percent of women age eighteen to thirty report being unhappy with their body size, 81 percent of ten-year-old girls report that they are afraid of being fat, and 42 percent of first to third grade girls say they want to be thinner. Men are also reporting discomfort with their body size and shape with 43 percent of men saying they want to be leaner and more muscular. Of course, these statistics are from self-reporters and can only give a partial view of the issue, but they aren't radically surprising.

To be labeled "fat" is often considered one of the most derogatory terms one can use toward someone else. Magazines displayed at the checkout line use body size and muscularity as a gauge to determine which celebrity is hot and who is not. We are taught that being fat is shameful and somehow indicative of our unworthiness, that we are only as good as our clothing size indicates, that no one will love us—and we shouldn't even love ourselves—if we are overweight.

Nonsense! It is difficult to combat the images and words that diminish our humanity in favor of our measurements, but that is precisely what self-esteem does. Every woman I know, including me, has tried diets and eating plans galore over the years, and you might have done so too. I have had numbers on the scale go up and down. I have worried and fretted about my weight. After decades of crazy-making negative self-talk, I have finally learned to love my body as it is, to eat the foods that contribute to my health and my happiness, and to know that my sexual self is worthy of care and celebration. You are just as deserving as anyone else.

There is a growing movement toward body acceptance for all sizes of people, and I encourage you to find role models who can guide you in loving your body with all your glorious curves, folds, and jiggly bits. Human bodies come in many shapes, and each one is wrapped around a soul that seeks connection and love.

Differently-abled bodies. No matter your age or your size, differently-abled bodies can also be challenging to self-esteem. If you have been living within a body that has restricted movement, limited communication, or cognitive differences, you likely have learned skills to adapt to the world that is designed primarily for people with fewer of those types of challenges. If you are a person whose body has changed in ability due to injury, surgery, or medication, you may not yet have learned these skills and you may not yet have come to mental acceptance about the changes in yourself. Self-esteem can feel far away in either case.

You can increase your self-esteem by noting your strengths, focusing on what you can do instead of what you cannot, and surrounding yourself with people who appreciate you as you are. If you are partnered, it is vital for both of you to speak openly and kindly about what you grieve losing—or never having—and what you admire and love about each other. Regardless of your abilities, you are lovable, desirable, and able to participate in sexual and sensual activities. Pleasure may look different for you than it does for others, and that's just fine. We are ever-changing beings, and the more we can move within those changes the better we feel about ourselves.

MARY'S STORY

I met Mary through mutual friends, and a few months later she contacted me about scheduling a session to talk about her sexual relationship with her husband. Her perception was that he wanted sex all the time, and while she loved him and wanted him to get his needs met, she didn't like it. She hoped that working with me would get her to a place where she could find some pleasure in sex and enjoy her husband.

During our first few sessions, I learned that Mary and her husband, William, had been married nearly twenty years. She revealed that she thought her body was disgusting because she was fat and that her vagina was "icky and gross." She avoided touching her genitals as much as possible. She did not allow herself to reach orgasm for fear of losing control. She was afraid to relax into her body much of the time, though she admitted liking to have some touch such as gentle back rubs and having her hair brushed. Mary said that she loved her husband very much and wanted him to be happy, so she gave in to William's pestering to have sex two to three times a week. She was afraid that William would leave her if she didn't please him, even though he always told her and spoke to others of his love for her and devotion to their marriage and had never suggested that he was going to leave. He knew that she wasn't getting much enjoyment from their sexual activity, but Mary kept assuring him that she wanted him to be happy, and she knew that receiving oral sex and having intercourse was pleasurable to him.

Mary told me that she had gone through weight-loss surgery several years before, and she had initially lost a significant amount of weight. She had gained much of it back through disregarding the eating protocol recommended by the doctor.

She did not attend any of the group support meetings suggested for her after surgery.

Mary claimed that she tried not to look in the mirror and avoided looking down at her body when she was showering. During sex, she would sometimes become too uncomfortable to continue because she felt her fat getting in the way or she became too focused on some part of her skin jiggling. She didn't like the stickiness of the lubricant that William had selected. Her overall enjoyment of anything sexual was close to nil.

Over the next couple of months, I encouraged her to pay attention to her internal monologue and to set an alarm on her phone to check in with her body several times each day. At each alarm, I asked her to take three slow breaths and scan her body. I wanted her to name her sensations, such as: "I feel tension in my chest." "My heart is beating very fast." "I'm feeling warmth in my feet and legs." I also asked her to try replacing any negative self-talk with a simple statement of acceptance that she wouldn't dismiss as a blatant lie. We worked on that one quite a bit as Mary revealed that she often heard her internal voice using words like "ugly," "hate," and "disgusting." I thought that Mary's mind would deny complete opposites like "beautiful," "love," and "wonderful," so I suggested she try to replace comments like "I'm so ugly" with "I like how my skin feels after I use lotion," and "I hate kissing" with "I enjoy William's gentleness" to encourage her to be gentler with her internal monologue and open the door to a more positive perspective.

She revealed her history of sexual trauma, and we started some exercises to break through the walls of protection she had built to shield herself from further hurt. Mary realized that she had started gaining weight when she met William and he revealed his sexual desire for her because her other "walls" weren't keeping him out. We talked extensively about how difficult and disorienting it is to want to be physically intimate with someone you love while also wanting to keep physical intimacy far away.

Mary began trying some of the exercises, like telling William that she wanted to participate in sexual activities on her terms. She wanted to experiment with pursuing him instead of always feeling pursued, which made her turn off. She also followed my suggestion of replacing the lubricant that she didn't like with coconut oil and found the sensation to be far more tolerable, even comfortable.

When I suggested she keep a journal to record her thoughts about her wishes and struggles, Mary said she didn't like to write things down because she was afraid that William or someone else would find and read her journal. She knew of someone who had found out information about a partner by reading emails, and she was afraid a similar unwanted disclosure would occur for her if she wrote down anything she was thinking or feeling. We talked several times about the benefits of having a method of getting her thoughts out and visible so that she could get some space from them and find some clarity or discover patterns of self-negating thoughts. Mary always came back to her fear of discovery as the reason for her reluctance in journaling. When I suggested that she may be reticent due to fear of what she would learn about herself, she agreed that might be true, yet she maintained her refusal to use journaling as a tool for self-exploration.

Mary was an intelligent and focused woman who had a successful career in a field she loved. She was used to being in charge, and she had crafted a life that allowed her to think and talk her way around most of her problems, or she simply locked them away and pretended they didn't exist. She was hurting emotionally, and her body was giving her signals that she was becoming physically unhealthy again; however, she decided not to continue with our sessions after a few months. She didn't believe me when I said she was worthy of love and care and enjoyment in her body and sexuality. She could hear my words, she was able to intellectually agree that people deserved to be happy and comfortable and feel good about themselves, but she wasn't able at that point to put herself in a place of feeling worthy and deserving of pleasure.

QUESTIONS FOR REFLECTION

What is your assessment of your physical attractiveness? What factors do you consider when assessing? Do you apply the same factors when assessing others?

Do you believe you are worthy of unconditional love, or do you believe you have to look or behave in a certain way in order to be loved?

Does your feeling of self-worth change often? If so, what are the factors that influence your self-esteem?

8

THE CARRY-ON:

ASK FOR WHAT YOU WANT

The field of asking is fundamentally improvisational. It thrives not in the creation of rules and etiquette but in the smashing of that etiquette.
—*Amanda Palmer*

WHEN WE TALK ABOUT SEXUAL DESIRE AS A CONCEPT, WE CAN affect a certain distance or objectivity and can usually offer some thoughts or facts based on our knowledge or experience about what people in general want and find enjoyable. However, when the conversation is focused on what *you* desire, and more specifically, what you desire with the other person in the conversation, then you must have a deeper level of trust. Trust in this area involves several aspects:

- Trusting yourself to know what you want, what turns you on, what your limits are, and what you are willing to try even if the idea makes you a bit nervous.
- Trusting in your ability to communicate with your partner in exploring new ideas, giving feedback on what you experience—both in the

moment and afterward—and using communication to deepen intimacy when you want to step into that.

- Trusting your partner to hear you without laughing at you, calling you names, or using judgmental language around your desires.
- Trusting that pleasure, feeling good together, and soul connecting are of paramount importance, that if either of you want to stop at any point, all action stops so that you can minimize discomfort and fear, followed by communication and actions for reconnection and rebuilding trust if needed.

Being honest about what you want is scary. What if the other person says no? What if they laugh at you? What if your desire brings up fear or disgust for your partner? It takes courage and love to be honest with yourself and with someone else. I believe that each baby step we take is important and should be celebrated. Every step leads you closer to your goal—whatever that may be—and gives you a track record of success to rely on when you feel unsure.

If talking about what you want is completely new, that's okay. Sometimes it takes a while to know what you do like, especially if you were raised with the mythology that your partner will just magically or intuitively know what you like and want at any given time—aka My-Life-Is-a-Movie syndrome. If you are unsure about all the things you like or might like, skip ahead to the Sexual Activities Checklist in the Appendix for a list of some activities that might spark your imagination and interest.

If asking for what you want goes against what you were given in your religious upbringing, you might be struggling with guilt or fear around "demanding" sex or putting an emphasis on pleasure. Those feelings are common among people, particularly women, who have been raised or lived for a while in a sexually restrictive faith tradition.

Here are some ways to get started with asking for what you want.

1. Talk to yourself.

Verbalizing your desires in your mind and then out loud allows you to practice saying things that are difficult. Try saying things in a different way each time to find what is most comfortable for you. Practice "talking dirty" so you can hear what that sounds like, which will help you to feel less awkward when saying those things with another person.

Actors do not walk on stage or on set with no idea of what to say. Even improvisational actors have a background of successful attempts to pull from when they are called to improvise a speech. Practicing gives you confidence!

2. Ask winning questions.

Winning questions are the kind that help both people to tune into each other and make it easy to say yes. This is the time to flex your consent muscles by asking for permission at every stage of connection. "May I hold your hand? Do you want me to rub your shoulders? May I kiss you?" Consent is supersexy!

This isn't just for people you are hooking up with for the first time either. When you're trying new things, it can be helpful to start with activities that are already "yes" activities so that you both get comfortable with doing things you both like. That way when you get to something new and feels like a stretch, you can know what a true yes feels like because you've been tuned into the yesses you've already experienced.

3. Give lots of praise and feedback.

Notice what you like: the things that make you want to say "yes" and "more" and "please don't stop." When your partner is doing those things, let them know! The more you can give your partner positive feedback for what they are doing, the more you build a base of trust for those times when you want to ask for something different.

Tune into your partner's tone of voice as well as the words. Listen for a change in breathing or small noises that indicate pleasure or discomfort. Watch facial expressions too. All this communication helps increase trust, which increases intimacy and the willingness to adventure together. When you are interested in your partner's pleasure as well as your own, it is easier to hear and respond to their verbal and nonverbal cues.

Tuning into pleasure short-circuits the ego response too. When we're concerned about performance, the ego gets defensive when someone else gives us suggestions and requests. Seeking perfection, wanting to achieve a certain position, or chasing an orgasm takes pleasure out of the picture, which doesn't make us feel good about sex.

By building a practice of noticing and commenting on the wonderful ways you feel pleasure and connection, your partner will be better able to hear you say "Yes, this, but not that." When you find that something isn't working as well for you, it's not hard to change gears and return to a guaranteed "yes" activity because you've already told them the things they do that you like.

4. Be willing to be silly.

Try something a bit silly, and see how it changes the mood. You don't have to do a comedy routine or a multilayered striptease in an animal costume, but trying a bit of goofiness can allow laughter to enter and open things up for experimenting. Be willing to look a little ridiculous and see how it increases your intimacy. Seeing our partner as human is a great relief because it allows us to be more fully human ourselves.

This also helps when you're trying something new or trying to fit your bodies together in a way that is novel or maybe more athletic or flexible than you're used to doing. It is easy to feel frustrated and nervous because we often tell ourselves that we have to do things perfectly or it breaks the mood or doesn't count. That's just not true. Perfection is rare, and even when you have years of experience with certain activities, you can run into times of "this just isn't working." Being willing to laugh it off and redirect the energy and focus into your connection can ease those times of potential embarrassment.

5. Talk about fantasies before you get into bed.

Having conversations about your fantasies and desires can be pretty scary. You're exposing your inner world, and for most of us, this opens up whole volumes of vulnerability. One way to increase confidence is to first talk about fantasies in a neutral area—not the bedroom—and at a neutral time—not right before having sex. It's very common for us to feel nervous, embarrassed, or even fearful of telling our deepest desires to someone else, no matter how much we think we can trust them. Go slowly. Start with something small. There's no gold star for going faster and feeling in danger.

If talking is difficult, try writing your turn-ons and fantasies in a relationship journal as a first step. Your partner can read what you wrote, and then you can start talking from there. With time and experience, you'll be able to talk about what you like, what you'd like to try, and what worked or didn't work in previous sex play without worrying about how your partner will react.

Reading erotica and watching sexy films can help you to learn what new things you'd like to try and what things are interesting to you. Some of us are more attuned to visual stimulation, some like to hear about sex—especially when a lover reads erotic stories—and some of us like the mental movies that happen when we read sexy writing or write it ourselves. Doing these activities together can be a wonderful way to explore new scenarios and situations that can fuel your adventurous side.

NOTE: Most pornography is not designed to promote intimacy or pleasure. The detriments of pornography are becoming more widely studied. Porn damages your brain and sexual responsiveness, negatively affects relationships, and leads to increased relationship violence—most often directed at women.

It is important to exercise extreme caution in consuming pornography that depicts violence, humiliation, or illegally involving children.

For stats and more information: fightthenewdrug.org.

6. Sexual Activities Checklist. *See Appendix for my suggested list.

Each partner will take a piece of paper and make a list of sexual activities that you have:

- experienced and liked
- experienced and not liked
- experienced and might like to do again in different circumstances
- not experienced and would like to try
- not experienced and don't want to try

Compare this list with your partner's list and talk about the similarities and differences. You both may want to try something new. Each of you may have something to teach the other. Remember when you are making your lists that sexual activity is anything that makes you feel sexy and gets you in the mood for intimate play. That seemingly innocent kiss or long look counts as a sexual activity if it gets you hot!

Now that you have some ideas for where to start in asking for what you want, let's talk about what exploration might bring up for you.

There is always the potential for discomfort when we try new things. I noted at the beginning of this chapter that it can be very scary to be honest about your desires. I come from a family in which sex was not discussed, and it took me a while to even ask questions around consent. Though I was fairly comfortable telling raunchy jokes because that was the way that my peers spoke, I wasn't used to using sexy language in an intimate setting or in a way that revealed my desires.

Discomfort with using unfamiliar language is one thing. Your discomfort with sexual activities can vary from mild nervousness to post-traumatic stress reactions due to unresolved traumas. If you have a history of sexual trauma (rape, sexual assault, sexualized bullying or harassment), please seek therapeutic support from a counselor who is trained to work with survivors. Even if you think you have worked through your past pain, a new lover might trigger your fight-or-flight response. It is very important for you and your partner to have lots of support as you navigate new territory in your sexual adventures.

In any new situation, you can always say no or not now. Your partner may also say no. You do not have to comply with another person's request for an activity you don't want to do. Being in a relationship means you make space for both the question and the response. The more you can talk about your desires, the greater capacity you both have for determining what activities you want to keep in your repertoire.

With patience, attention, and caring, learning to ask for what you want can feel empowering. You'll be learning more about yourself and your partner, which will allow you to let go of experiences of pain and reclaim your sexuality and pleasure. Your soul connection with your partner becomes stronger because you are building greater trust and acceptance. It all starts with knowing what you like and what you'd like to experience together. The biggest result is a deeper spiritual connection with yourself and your partner.

How I Learned to Ask for What I Want

For the first decade of my sexual and relationship life, I definitely had the My-Life-Is-a-Movie syndrome! I thought that the magic of sexual desire and the "natural" connection of dating someone would negate the need for communication and that any person I was with would just intuitively know what my body liked and how to bring me pleasure. Of course, the fact that I didn't know what I liked, nor was I sure what someone else liked, didn't compute with my fantasy of the perfect lover.

I started verbalizing a few desires during my late twenties with my husband, and I believe he tried his best given our ages and inhibitions around talking about sex. He always stopped when I asked, but I often didn't ask. I just gritted my teeth and endured the discomfort because I didn't want him to think he was a bad lover. I'd learned in my sexual experiences before I met him that I shouldn't ever let a guy think he was a bad lover, or else. The "or else" part was my fear of being labeled a slut for knowing "too much" about sex at a young age and my greater fear of male violence that can happen when the ego perceives insult. I also had my own misunderstandings surrounding the dichotomy and connection between pleasure and orgasm.

After we split up in my early thirties, I found lovers who listened to me and asked me what I wanted. I dated people who allowed for the exploration of pleasure without the pressure to have every experience end with a mind-blowing orgasm... or the need for orgasm at all. Pleasure was the goal, and if everyone felt good, the sex was good too.

One of my lovers taught me that I could relax and simply receive pleasure without immediately thinking and planning on how to reciprocate. She used lots of questions and opportunities for consent so that I felt safe and cared for even as we explored new and exciting activities. She allowed me to go slowly, to stop and breathe, to stay in touch with my body. We talked about how she liked to be touched, what activities I liked, and what fantasies we wanted to play out.

One of my lovers taught me that oral sex can be pleasurable for the giver as well as the receiver. She convinced me that my natural smell and taste wasn't gross or weird, and her sounds of pleasure in giving allowed me to find nuances in my own pleasure because I didn't worry that she was secretly hoping I'd have a fast orgasm so that she could be done. She taught me that long, slow, sensual play was a worthy activity that didn't have to end in orgasm. We learned new ways of talking about sex and pleasure that helped me with subsequent lovers. Together we explored Taoist and other styles of spiritual sexuality that brought us closer energetically as well as physically.

In 2015, when I met the woman who is now my wife, I was forty-three; she was forty-five. We both came to our relationship with full and varied sexual and relationship histories. We were both grateful that we had lots of experience with other lovers and that we could talk about those experiences without feeling judged or inadequate. We used all our skills to build trust with each other: using consent, focusing on pleasure, talking about what we liked and didn't like, checking in often while exploring new activities, giving lots of feedback and nonverbal cues to indicate pleasure, and stopping when the other person expressed hesitation or discomfort. Our sexual connection is strong not only because we have great chemistry but also because we continue to build trust by communicating our desires and feelings before, during, and after sex. We want what's best for each other and for the benefit of our spiritual connection. We have a very broad definition of sex so that we don't get stuck in a rut of thinking that sex can only look a certain way, which is very helpful now that we are both experiencing libido shifts and sensation differences brought about by the process of menopause and the hormonal changes this stage of life brings.

Once I learned that my sexual and relationship satisfaction was mostly my responsibility, I knew I could increase that satisfaction by increasing my communication around what I liked, what I wanted, and how I desired to be touched. Pleasure became my indicator of success: Did I like how I felt? Did I enjoy being with the person I was with? Did my body feel comfortable, energized, expansive? Did I trust that my lover would respond to my requests? Did I feel safe to explore new activities? All these questions helped me to understand what I enjoy and expect in sexual—and nonsexual—relationships.

QUESTIONS FOR REFLECTION

Do I know what I like?

Can I talk about my desires with my current partner?

How does it feel to imagine asking for what I want in a new situation?

9

THE WEEKENDER:

SEX AS A SPIRITUAL PRACTICE

Your soul is your connection to the Divine. Sacred sex is an activity of joining souls in holy, celestial creation, expressing your appreciation for the gift of life, of sharing your body's vitality with another.
—*Brownell Landrum*

WHEN YOU HEAR THE WORDS "SPIRITUAL PRACTICE," WHAT COMES to mind? Do you think of prayer, of singing hymns or chanting, of meditation, of listening to a priest or minister, of participating or watching some sort of ritual, or something else completely? Perhaps this is a new concept for you, and you're not sure what to think.

For me, spiritual practice is the art and dedication to living my life fully aware of my soul while also fully present in my body and with my emotions. This means that whatever I am doing can be a spiritual practice. I can be talking with a friend and feeling the joy of connection, not trying to rush away to do the next thing or lose the conversation in thinking of the past mistakes I've made. This is a spiritual practice. I can be arguing with my lover and staying present to the uncomfortable feelings that arise from being in conflict, and this, too, is a spiritual practice. I can be doing the dishes, listening to music, taking a shower, shopping for groceries, checking my bank balance, and if I remain present in my body, aware of my connection to the universe and all beings and accepting whatever emotions and thoughts come up in the moment, it is a spiritual practice.

Likewise, sexual contact and conversation can also be a spiritual practice when we remain fully present in our bodies, aware of our connection to our souls, and communicating about our emotions, especially if those emotions might create a barrier or pull our focus away from the moment. The thing to remember about spiritual practice is that it is a practice, not a perfection. We get to keep practicing and treating ourselves with loving compassion during those times when we miss the mark.

The biggest problem for most of us when thinking about sex as a spiritual practice is that we've been told by our families, our cultures, and our religions that sex and spirituality cannot, and usually should not, exist in the same moment. We have been told that we are to deny our body and its animalistic needs and desires. We have been told that truly spiritual people don't focus on bodily desires but transcend the body in favor of the mind and soul.

Unpacking the baggage of what culture and family and religion contain concerning sexuality can be difficult because it is often linked strongly with shame, especially for women. Under patriarchal systems, women have historically been blamed for men's sexual desires as well as men's sexual transgressions or inabilities. People who are attracted to people of the same sex have also been targeted as sinful, shameful, dangerous, and damaged. As I've written in previous chapters, shame is powerful because it attacks our essence and tells us that we are not good enough to deserve to be loved. If we have been told that sexuality and desire takes us away from divinity/God, then we can be made vulnerable to feeling dirty and shameful for wanting to follow the pleasures found in sexual contact with ourselves and with others.

Spiritual Sex Practices From Around the World

Many Eastern spiritual traditions embrace sexual expression and intercourse as a healthy and vital part of life as well as a connection between humans and the divine. There are spiritual practices within these religions, especially non-monotheistic religions, that deliberately celebrate sexuality and sexual connection. You might have heard of the *Kama Sutra*, an ancient book that depicts multiple positions for sexual pleasure. This comes out of the Hindu tradition. Tantra Yoga, a practice of breathing and sensual touch to prolong arousal, is also an aspect of Hinduism. Many Wiccans and other pagan religions acknowledge the Great Rite in which a priestess and priest of a coven embody the Goddess and the God in sexual union, though in some groups this is only symbolized with ritual tools of the chalice (a bowl or cup representing the receptive female principle) and the athame (a ritual dagger representing the directive male principle), rather than with actual intercourse. In Taoism, there is also a tradition of sexual practices designed to connect the spirits of the individuals and use sexual energy, known as jing, to enhance overall bodily energy or chi.

Hindu Sexual Practices

When it comes to literature on sex practices, the *Kama Sutra of Vatsayana*, written in the second century (between 100–200CE), is the oldest known writing still in use today. It has detailed explanations and beautiful drawings that explain various ways in which a man can entice and pleasure a woman and how a woman can attract and pleasure a man. It even has guidelines for including more than two participants as well as instructions for marriage, social mores, and creating a home.

This book was translated from Sanskrit into English in the late 1800s by an Indian archaeologist and a British civil servant who were assisted by an Indian student. It is believed to be the oldest study of human sexuality and sexual sociology. It not only depicts sexual positions, but it discusses the value of arousal through kissing, embracing, and sensual touch prior to intercourse. The author often uses the phrase "This is learned by practice." This repetition is a reminder that sharing physical pleasure through sex is not something that you see in a picture or read about once and are suddenly a master lover. This kind of practice is what makes loving fun!

A somewhat more recent spiritual sexual practice is Tantric Yoga. While this type of yoga can involve specific poses or asanas, like a more traditional yoga practice, in Tantra there is a heightened focus on the prana or breath. Practitioners are encouraged to use specific breathing styles coupled with sensual sexual touch to increase sexual arousal. More than simply focusing on breathing, though, Tantric Yoga teaches us to use our bodies and the bliss that comes from sexual connection to connect to source energy or the divine.

Taoist Sexual Practices

The slow, meditative body exercise known as Qi Gong has been practiced for centuries by people in China. With several spelling variations such as qigong, chi kung, or chi gung, it can be confusing for English speakers. However, all of these spellings refer to the same holistic system of posture, movement, breathing, and meditation which is translated as "Life Energy Cultivation." This practice is used to enhance chi or life energy in all areas: physical health, mental awareness, and spiritual connection.

Sexual energy is called *jing* in this Chinese tradition. Taoist sexual practices talk of using jing as a way to enhance *chi*. Men are encouraged not to have too many orgasms, which can diminish their chi by wasting their jing through excess seminal expulsion. Mantak Chia is one of the foremost recognized teachers of Taoist sexual practices. He, and others like him, advocate that men retain their seminal fluid by learning to hold back on orgasm and use that sexual energy to fortify their life force. Women, in this practice, are said to lose life force through menstruation and childbearing, and that they, too, can use sexual energy to enhance health and well-being. Within this practice, people are taught the way to move energy throughout the body using the "microcosmic orbit." In very simple terms, energy flows from the perineum, up the spine, over the top of the head to the roof of the mouth; there is also another energy stream that flows up the front of the body through all the organs. By focusing on the breath while touching the tongue to the roof of the mouth, a person can help the energy to flow in a circuit up the back and down the front, which helps to clear energy blockages.

When two people are sexually intimate, they can enhance their microcosmic orbits by breathing together and directing energy to flow from the genitals up into and throughout the body. Taoist sexual practices do not talk of shame but of lost or mis-used energy. The focus of sex as a spiritual practice is in using our very human desires for sexual connection as a way to increase life energy.

Wiccan Great Rite

Wiccans may seem to be a religious group that all believe the same tenets, but that is not the case. There are nearly as many types of Wiccans as there are types of Christians. Several sects of Wiccans and other pagan traditions, however, do agree on the holy ritual of the Great Rite. Often part of Beltane (May 1) celebrations but sometimes used during other rituals as well, the Great Rite is the uniting of the sacred feminine and sacred masculine energies. Many times this is done symbolically with an athame (sacred dagger or knife), representing the God/sacred male energy, placed inside a chalice (sacred cup) filled with wine or ale, representing the Goddess/sacred female energy. The athame is then stirred in a clockwise direction.

With some groups, a priestess and a priest embody the Goddess and the God and engage in sexual intercourse as part of the ritual celebration. For ancient peoples, there were often sacred marriages in which a priestess would embody the Goddess who represented the land and a chieftain or king would represent the people of the tribe. This sexual ritual, called the *Hieros Gamos*, showed that the people were not separated from the land and worked together for the fertility and prosperity of the land and the tribe.

Traditional Jewish Teachings

Judaism is generally quite positive about sex for married people, regarding it as a divine gift and a holy obligation—both for the purposes of procreation and for pleasure and intimacy. The Talmud specifies that a husband is not only required to be intimate with his wife, but sources also indicate that he is obliged to sexually satisfy her. So vital is sexual activity considered to Judaism that celibacy, even for those so devoted to spiritual life that they feel they don't have energy left for marriage and children, is frowned upon.

That doesn't mean anything goes for observant Jews. Instead, sexual activity is highly circumscribed in Jewish tradition, as the rabbis of the Talmud sought to use the human libido as a tool for increasing the population and strengthening marriage. Traditional Jewish law not only prohibits many types of sexual relationships, but it also dictates specific parameters even for the permitted ones. And while Judaism is broadly permissive when it comes to sex between married adults, the same is not true for sexual activity outside a committed relationship.

The one place where sexuality is intrinsically sacred is in the poetry of "The Song of Songs." The writer speaks of divine love as intimately as with a human lover, and the celebration of erotic pleasure is central to the message.

Modern Practices Created Out of Ancient Wisdom

In the past twenty years, countries in the Western Hemisphere and beyond have seen a rise in sex educators, teachers, gurus, and speakers who are using ancient techniques and modern technologies to reach people who are fed up with feeling shamed and repressed about their sexuality. Many of these new practices share similarities though they may focus on slightly different aspects of spirituality and sex.

Mindfulness. Centering awareness on different body parts, going slowly.

Breath work/Breathing practices. Easy to practice solo or with another, play with breathing patterns and focusing attention on different body parts and increase arousal.

Focused masturbation. A way to explore your own divine sexuality and learn how to open yourself to working with divine energy before and between sharing that energy with a partner. At all stages of spiritual practice, you begin with yourself. Being whole in yourself and leaning into pleasure with no expectation of a certain outcome, you can become confident in what you like and want and learn how to get it.

Abstinence. Choosing to be sexually intimate with only yourself or choosing to redirect sexual energy for a while and put it into another creative endeavor or spiritual practice.

Seeing the divine in the other. Not only a sex practice but a way of being in a relationship that encourages practitioners to remember that we are all sparks of the divine source.

Divine Eros. Some Christian therapists and teachers such as Rollo May and Chuck MacKnee have used the term "divine eros" to describe sexual pleasure as connected to God. In *The Soul of Sex*, Thomas Moore, a former Catholic monk, explores the role of sex as a soulful—and soul-filled—experience.

Sex Magick. Using sexual energy (solo or shared) for the purpose of adding energy to a spell or prayer.

Kink/BDSM. BDSM stands for bondage and discipline, domination and submission, and sadism and masochism. The term "kink" is a sort of shorthand to describe sharing intense physical experiences by contracted (verbal or written) mutual agreement that involve communicated consent, deep trust, regular check-in, and mindfulness. While kink is portrayed as demeaning and disgusting by some people, I have learned through observation and participation that any act that involves willing consent, tender care, and honest communication can also be a vehicle of transformation and transcendence: true connection with divine energy. Many people who participate in kink as part of their sexual encounters speak openly and reverently about overcoming shame, learning to ask for what they want, setting clear boundaries about what is off-limits, and finding peace and comfort through the intensity of the sensations produced by the activities.

In myriad iterations of sacred sexuality, the common themes center on breathing, awareness, honesty, and presence. When we show up with our whole selves, and we sincerely seek to connect to another with body, thought, emotion, and soul, we can find the integration and expansion that can only be experienced in connection with another person. Does that mean that every spiritual sexual experience is mind-blowing or takes us to dizzying levels of passionate ecstasy? Probably not.

We are human, after all, and we are bound to have ebbs and flows in all our energies. The point is to continue to be aware of who we are and who we want to be as divine humans in our relationships and then to be compassionate and forgive ourselves when we don't quite reach our ideals.

TYRONE AND MICHAEL

When Tyrone and his partner, Michael, booked their first session, they were clear that their relationship was mostly satisfying but had lost some of the zing they had enjoyed in the beginning. They wanted to talk about ways to enhance their sexual intimacy, and they also wanted to explore what it would mean to open up their relationship and date other people while also maintaining their partnership. Tyrone was very certain about wanting to only be sexual with men, while Michael had identified as bisexual all his life. They were both in their late forties and had been together for three years.

During our first session, both men talked about their likes and turn-ons, the varied activities they had explored with each other, and the ways in which they had learned to honor boundaries and communicate their needs. We talked about my theory of the rhythm of relationships: the first year is often about telling our stories, the highlights and generally humorous lowlights that we think will best entice and retain a lover, the second year is about nesting and building a world of couplehood, and year three is the call to deeper intimacy that usually challenges us to show up in a more vulnerable way.

Michael and Tyrone were right in the messy middle of that call to deeper intimacy. While they had worked on their communication using some tools and guidance that I provided in our sessions, the real work for them was to decide how deep into intimacy they wanted to go. One of my suggestions to them was to read a book about Taoist sexual practices and explore seminal retention, the microcosmic orbit, and moving energy from one to the other using the breath.

For several weeks, it seemed to be going well with Tyrone and Michael. Their sessions were filled with talk of discoveries and pleasures. They expressed satisfaction with the practices and talked of feeling a new sense of falling in love.

One day, however, I received a phone call from Tyrone to tell me that he and Michael were not going to be attending our scheduled session the following day and that they had decided to open up their relationship in order to date other people. I asked if they had come up against something negative or uncomfortable in their homework, but Tyrone would not say why they were canceling other than to reiterate that they wanted to explore dating others. I wished them well and kept the door open for future work, but I never heard from them again. I wondered if the openness was a mutual choice or if one partner had given the other an ultimatum of dating others or breaking up. I have found that some couples choose to explore polyamory or open relationship as a way to avoid diving deeper into intimacy.

JAKE AND NADIA

Jake and Nadia got together at a "play party," a semiprivate gathering of people interested in one or more aspects of BDSM or kink as a part of their sexuality. In this case, semiprivate meant that although there was a private invitation list, the event was held in a public venue, and invitees were allowed to bring a guest who might not have been listed on the invitation. Both Jake and Nadia were fairly new to kink and were eager to explore a wide range of activities, primarily with Jake in the dominant role and Nadia in the submissive role.

Jake was a twenty-four-year-old self-described bookworm. He loved to research and read about new activities and interests. Nadia was twenty-two and had been in a long-term relationship with a woman for two years, though they'd broken up a few months before she met Jake. Both were drawn to the sensuality of bondage experiences and were interested in learning about how to be safe and risk-aware while also exploring new skills. During our sessions, we talked about their previous sexual experiences, their familiarity with kink practices, and what writing a contract could entail.

Nadia had one experience of being part of a scene—a preplanned encounter that may or may not involve sexual contact, in which all members consent to the plan prior to any action—several months before the party where she met Jake. She reported that her scene partner had used spanking and hair pulling along with slower sensual touches to build arousal and that it was incredibly cathartic for her to reach a level of intensity that brought about tears, yells, and powerful energy in the form of shuddering orgasm through her body. Because she trusted her play partner to care for her and check in with her throughout the scene, she told me that she felt clearer, fresher, and more spiritually integrated when it was over and she had time to reflect on it.

Jake had dated two different women who were curious about kink, and together they explored sensual experiences like spanking, hot-and-cold play, and blindfolding. While he didn't talk about his experience with those encounters as specifically spiritual, he did talk of the awe he felt for each partner's willingness to place her trust in him.

I worked with Nadia and Jake for nearly eight months, and in that time they explored finding a community of other kinksters through online forums and real-time play parties. They wrote a contract that had a definite end date of six months and listed all the agreements they were making for time spent together, activities they would explore, and the ways they would care for each other before, during, and after each experience. They also included agreements for regular check-ins with me so that they would have a neutral space to bring up concerns.

The contract did not address what would happen if one or both of them grew to have deeper feelings of love and attachment, and ultimately that was the piece that caused the greatest difficulty when the contract was over. Nadia wanted to continue dating Jake, but Jake was ready for their relationship to take a break so that he could get back to focusing on his graduate studies. At our last session, they talked about this shift and did their best to honor each other and their different desires while also staying centered in their own feelings. Each of them used language of spirituality, such as expanded consciousness, increased awe, and heart healing to describe their time together and the deep appreciation they had for each other. They found, through the intensity of their kink play, a deeper and more satisfying connection and a spiritual consciousness that they didn't anticipate on the outset.

HANNA AND JASMINE

I met Hanna and Jasmine at a women's spiritual gathering. They were both training to be tantra practitioners to assist women in learning how to move sexual energy from a strictly genital focus into the rest of the body. They were also lovers and had been together for almost seven years. They had discovered tantra as part of their desire to undo their patterns of running away from intimacy in previous relationships. They asked me if I would work with them to integrate more awareness of their tantra spirituality into their everyday relationship.

I remember being surprised that they were such a long-term couple because they were both so independent. They each laughed at that. Hanna explained that she was glad I noticed because they'd been working on being independent and interdependent for a few years. Jasmine added that they had made a commitment to each other to foster each other's independence as part of their commitment to being a couple. Hanna was thirty-six with long braids and a muscular frame. She had been married to a man for a few years in her early twenties. Jasmine was thirty-two and spoke with a soft and calm voice. She said she had a couple of relationships in high school and college in which she felt she let herself get lost in the other woman's wants and needs before meeting Hanna. Because of their experiences in previous relationships, they felt that setting out clear expectations in the beginning would keep them from repeating the behaviors they saw as mistakes.

Like many people who start with the best of intentions, Jasmine and Hanna did well in the beginning in not repeating their codependent patterns. By the fifth year of the relationship, however, Hanna noticed that Jasmine was quieter and less forthcoming about her feelings and wants. When challenged, Jasmine brushed Hanna's concerns away, saying that everything was fine. The trouble came to the surface just after their fifth anniversary when Hanna's family announced a large reunion in another state. Jasmine did not want to attend, but she allowed Hanna to make the plans for the two of them. Two days before they were to leave, Jasmine started an argument over whether to use one suitcase or two, and the tension escalated into shouting and blaming with Jasmine finally stating that she hadn't wanted to go to the reunion from the beginning.

They talked deeply about what had happened and agreed to read a book about intimacy together. That book had led them to the practice of tantra and the awareness of spiritual sexual practices. Hanna talked about how their sex life had improved dramatically and that tantric energy practices were helping to keep their intimacy going for several hours after each experience. What they were currently experiencing was the challenge of remaining intimate and connected during disagreements.

I started by having them talk about a recent argument, using an example of something small that they had mostly worked through—Jasmine's habit of leaving her shoes by the door in such a way that Hanna regularly tripped over them. At that point Hanna had somewhat resigned herself to moving

Jasmine's shoes on a daily basis, but she still wasn't happy about it.

Using a technique I have developed called "I Got Your Back," I asked them to stand back-to-back and lean just a little bit on the other. I instructed them to think about the argument, about the feelings they each had regarding the shoes by the door. After a minute, I asked what they noticed about the other person's back. Jasmine said she forgot to notice Hanna's presence because she was focused on her side of the shoe argument. Hanna said she first noted that Jasmine's back got tense but then she, too, had focused solely on her own feelings and irritation in remembering the disagreement. We talked about exercising both the ability to stay centered in yourself and the ability to tune into your partner. I encouraged them to pay attention to each other and start again with recalling the argument silently.

This time, when asked, each woman reported that she noticed how tense the other's back had become after just a few breaths. We worked on breathing and relaxing muscle tension for a few minutes, and then, while still standing back-to-back, I told Jasmine to talk about her perspective of the shoe argument. Hanna's job was simply to breathe, listen, and notice what happened in Jasmine's back as she was speaking. Then they switched roles with Jasmine listening, breathing, and noticing while Hanna spoke about her view of the argument. When Jasmine began to cry a little, I encouraged her to lean into Hanna a bit more. When Hanna felt Jasmine's extra pressure, she increased her pressure in return.

When they were done speaking, we talked about the experience of holding each other up. They both expressed how they had been able to feel the other person's tension in talking about the irritation, but they had also felt supported and heard in a whole new way.

I explained that the support is part of the power of this

technique. While there are a few more components, the essential act of knowing that you can speak your truth without worrying how you look or if you'll react to the other person's facial expression, combined with the encouragement to feel all the feelings and the physical sensation of your partner still "having your back," can break through the walls of defense that we put up during a disagreement. Over the next few sessions, we worked on practicing what they learned with small irritations and applying that to larger, deeper discomforts. Using the practice of breathing that is used in tantra to spread and enhance sexual energy, Jasmine and Hanna were able to breathe and tune into their desire to connect and resolve disagreements and return to a state of ease and intimacy.

QUESTIONS FOR REFLECTION

What were you told about sex and spirit or about sex and religious experiences?

How can you reclaim your divine right to bodily pleasure and sexual fulfillment?

What does integrating sexuality and spirituality mean for you?

10

THE SATCHEL:

WHAT'S LEFT IN YOUR BAG?

He who would travel happily must travel light.
—Antoine De Saint-Exupéry

SATCHELS ARE FAIRLY SMALL. BY NOW YOU MAY BE READY AND able to pare down your baggage and decide what is important for you to take with you as you move forward on your embodied spiritual journey of life and relationships.

Your experiences and perceptions have brought you to this point, and they are important touchstones for you to use when you come up against new challenges, new relationships, and deeper intimacy. What you've learned in your life's journey informs how you meet what waits ahead, but that information is not all that helps you to respond when you are challenged. You now have some emotional and spiritual tools to unpack the baggage you have carried that holds your experiences and the thoughts and feelings that are part of them. You can use what you've learned in this book to bring a wider perspective on how you allow those experiences to influence your future behavior in intimate relationships.

Here's what I hope you'll take with you in your small satchel:

- Comfort and ease in owning your baggage, claiming your wisdom, honoring your soul and your path of learning with all the pain, bias, and expectations you've uncovered while also doing your best to understand how all of your luggage can fit in or clash with someone else's trunks and bags.
- Realization that painful experiences in your past might have influenced your decisions and actions but that you can retrain your brain to expect and accept more pleasurable experiences of learning because you know about neuroplasticity. You can shift your thought patterns to be aware of your current situations and not operate from unconscious programming.
- Ability to question your assumptions and let go of all the "shoulds" that others have given you to carry.
- Cultivating your presence, mentally, physically, and spiritually while de-emphasizing performance in sexual relationships; learning to drop the mask of who you think you need to be in order to please others and tune into what she or he says and shows you they want.
- Understanding your own definition of satisfaction.
- Loving and caring for your body in all its beauty and imperfection; disregard for other people's judgment about your looks or abilities; celebration of what your body can do and feel that brings you pleasure, and appreciation for the differences each lover will bring to your life.
- Strength to ask for what you want and acceptance that sometimes your lover will say no to your request; using techniques to practice asking for what you want and saying no to what you don't want; taking

responsibility for your own orgasm, if you want to have one.

- Honoring of your spiritual sexual self. You are not only allowed to blend your divinity with your humanity; your joy and growth depend on your full integration of your mind, body, and spirit.

Don't think that you have to forget or throw away everything that has come before now. Paring down baggage doesn't mean you don't have some trunks of memories and experiences that you've packed away for reference. You don't throw away the old you; you embrace how your past fits into your present. This understanding gives you the spaciousness to accept and celebrate all of yourself. This spaciousness allows you to choose how you show up in each situation. So often, we diminish ourselves so that we only express a small portion of who we are. I know that each of us is a multidimensional and complex being. We are prisms catching light and shadow, reflecting both our internal selves and interacting with the environment around us.

When we can acknowledge and embrace being a prismatic human, we come to understand that we have myriad ways of expressing ourselves. Different facets come through at different times and situations. This awareness of being prismatic helps us to get comfortable with the fact that we will probably never be fully known even to ourselves and therefore we can understand that we'll never fully know our partners either. Keeping this sacred mystery in our minds, we can overcome the tendency to label ourselves or our partners as boring. Having curiosity for what hasn't yet been discovered or revealed is one of the best tools for the journey of relationships.

It is time to lighten your load. You've carried this heavy mismatched luggage long enough. I know it can be exhausting to imagine all the unpacking, but you don't have to do everything at once. One step at a time—examining one bag, one old and flawed view of yourself, one pattern of behavior that no longer works for you, is all you need to focus on for now. You can find help through counseling, journaling, meditation and prayer, and talking with friends who are also seeking to unpack their own baggage.

In this journey of lightening up, I wish you joy and peace, love and adventure and wisdom, and most of all, the true integration of your spiritual sexual self so that you continue to learn, love, and become all of who you truly are.

ABOUT THE AUTHOR

Rev. DiAnna Ritola is a sex educator and counselor, Interfaith Minister, and Dianic Wiccan Priestess who has been studying, speaking, and practicing at the intersections of spirituality and sexuality as they come alive in intimate relationships since 2007. She advocates releasing shame associated with sexuality, body image, and sex and religion to celebrate the joy and adventure of embodiment through reclaiming our birthright as spiritual sexual beings.

She counsels individuals and couples in her private practice, facilitates workshops for groups, and is in demand as a dynamic and engaging speaker at events throughout the United States.

DiAnna lives in New York City with her wife, Michele Fitzsimmons, their cat, Lilith, and their dog, Brigid. Her two daughters, Mira and Ila, who still occasionally roll their eyes at their mom, also live in NYC.

facebook.com/Rev-Di-Anna-Ritola-1454152664810933
instagram.com/rev_di

SEXUAL ACTIVITIES CHECKLIST

Use the list below to discover your likes and dislikes, your fantasies and desires, and to kick start your sexual conversations.

Beside each activity, put the number that best describes your experience with it. Then use the information to share your desires with a partner.

Rating

1= Experienced and liked it

2= Experienced and didn't like it

3= Experienced and might like to do it again in a different circumstance

4= Not experienced but want to try

5= Not experienced and don't want to

6= I'm not sure (use this as infrequently as possible)

This is not an exhaustive list! Please feel free to add things as you need or want to make this list about you. This is your tool to greater openness in your sexual conversations. Make it personal.

Activities that can be performed while clothed
__Looking into another person's eyes
__Matching your breathing with another person
__Holding hands in the car
__Holding hands in public
__Walking arm in arm
__Licking someone's neck or ear
__Having your neck or ear licked
__Biting above the shoulders
__Running hands through a partner's hair
__Braiding or brushing hair
__Giving / receiving scalp massage
__Being bitten above the shoulders
__Kissing—mouth closed
__Kissing—mouth open
__Kissing face/ears/neck/hair
__Spooning while sleeping
__Finger sucking—giving/receiving
__Giving/receiving massage of shoulders or back
__Giving/receiving foot massage
__Giving/receiving full-body massage
__Verbal sharing of fantasies
__Giving/receiving a lap dance
__Performing a striptease
__Holding partner's face in your hands/touching partner's face with fingertips
__Watching a sexually stimulating film alone
__Watching a sexually stimulating film together
__Reading erotic literature alone
__Reading erotic literature together

Clothing off or Clothing Optional Activities
__Toe/foot sucking or kissing

__Breast/nipple stimulation

__Using a vibrator alone

__Using a vibrator with partner

__Sexual intercourse missionary position—penis/vagina

__Sexual intercourse missionary position—penis/anus

__Sexual intercourse missionary position—dildo/vagina

__Sexual intercourse missionary position—dildo/anus

__Fingers inserted in vagina—giving/receiving

__Fingers inserted in anus—giving/receiving

__Genital stimulation with mouth/tongue (cunnilingus/fellatio) giving/receiving

__Anal stimulation with tongue (anilingus) giving/receiving

__Light touching on skin with feather or fabric

__Giving/receiving spanking

__Giving/receiving flogging, caning, or whipping

__Clitoral stimulation with hand/finger

__Clitoral stimulation with vibrator/dildo

__Sexual Intercourse doggy style

__Sexual Intercourse cowgirl style

__Sexual Intercourse reverse cowgirl

__Bathing/showering with partner

__Being washed by partner—partner outside of tub

__Having hair washed by partner

__Sleeping nude alone

__Sleeping nude with partner

__Masturbation

__Masturbation with a partner (mutual masturbation)

__Masturbation while partner watches

__Group sexual activity (more than two people)

__Voyeurism: watching others engage in sexual activity—live not film

__Role-playing

__Costumes

__Sexual intercourse—side by side spooning

__Sexual intercourse—giver on side, receiver partially on back

__Sexual intercourse—other _____

RESOURCES FOR READERS

Books

Conscious Loving: The Journey to Co-Commitment by Gay Hendricks, PhD and Kathlyn Hendricks, PhD

Codependent No More: How to Stop Controlling Others and Start Caring by Melody Beattie

Eight Dates by John Gottman, PhD and Julie Schwartz Gottman, PhD

Eye Movement Desensitization and Reprocessing (EMDR) Therapy by Francine Shapiro, PhD

Getting the Love you Want: A Guide for Couples by Harville Hendrix, PhD

Healing Love Through the Tao: Cultivating Female Sexual Energy by Mantak Chia

Kama Sutra of Vatsayana

Mary Magdalene Revealed by Meggan Watterson

Mating in Captivity: Unlocking Erotic Intelligence by Esther Perel

Taoist Secrets of Love by Mantak Chia with Michael Winn

The Brain that Changes Itself by Dr. Norman Doidge, MD.

The Seven Principles for Making Marriage Work by John M. Gottman, PhD

Waking the Tiger: Healing Trauma by Peter A. Levine and Ann Frederick

Women's Anatomy of Arousal: Secret Maps to Buried Pleasure by Sheri Winston, CNM, RN, BSN, LMT

Websites

drarielleschwartz.com - Somatic Therapy. Arielle Schwartz, PhD

fightthenewdrug.org - Studies on the impact of pornography on individuals, couples, and society

health.cornell.edu/sites/health.files/pdf-library/sensate-focus.pdf Sensate Focus exercise. Masters & Johnson

healthline.com - What Does It Mean to Be Touch Starved. Lauren Sharkey with Janet Brito, PhD, LCSW,CST

lovewithoutlimits.com - Tantra, Polyamory. Deborah Taj Anapol, PhD